I0359877

THOMAS M. TWIGG JR.

CRUSHED

FINDING HOPE
AND HEALING
AFTER TRUST
IS BROKEN

Copyright © 2025 Thomas M. Twigg, Jr.

All rights reserved. No part of this publication may be reproduced, distributed, or transmitted in any form or by any means, including photocopying, recording, or other electronic or mechanical methods, without the prior written permission of the publisher, except in the case of brief quotations embodied in critical reviews and certain other noncommercial uses permitted by copyright law. For permission requests, write to the publisher, addressed "Attention: Permissions Coordinator," to info@arrowpresspublishing.com

Paperback: 978-1-951475-44-4
E-book: 978-1-951475-45-1

Library of Congress Control Number: 2025910172

First paperback edition: July 2025

Accounts in this book are written to the truest recollection of the author's memory. Some names, places, and identifying details have been changed to protect privacy.

Scripture quotations marked NKJV are taken from the New King James Version®. Copyright © 1982 by Thomas Nelson. Used by permission. All rights reserved.

cripture quotations marked (ESV) are from The ESV® Bible (The Holy Bible, English Standard Version®), © 2001 by Crossway, a publishing ministry of Good News Publishers. Used by permission. All rights reserved.

Scripture quotations marked (KJV) are from the King James Version, Public Domain

Arrow Press Publishing
Summerville, SC 29486

www.arrowpresspublishing.com

CONTENTS

FOREWORD 9

INTRODUCTION 11

PART ONE: DEALING WITH FEELINGS 17

ANGER 21

JEALOUSY 26

BITTERNESS 27

DEPRESSION 28

HOPELESSNESS 30

GUILT 32

BLAME 35

HURT	35
DISBELIEF	37
DISGUST	38
SHAME	40
EMBARRASSMENT	44
FEAR	45
ANXIETY	47
PANIC	51
LONELINESS	52
BETRAYED	58
SHOCKED	58
HATE	59
REVENGE	61
OVERWHELMED	63
STRESSED	64
MOURNING	66

PART TWO: DEFINING INFIDELITY   69

PHYSICAL/SEXUAL FIDELITY	71

EMOTIONAL INFIDELITY	74
ONE NIGHT SEXUAL FLING	79
FRIENDS WITH BENEFITS	81
CYBER INFIDELITY	82
PORNOGRAPHY—THE NEW INFIDELITY	83
SEXTING	89

PART THREE: DEALING WITH HEALING — 91

STEPS OF EMOTIONAL HEALING	94
STEPS OF PSYCHOLOGICAL HEALING	104
STEPS OF SPIRITUAL HEALING	115
STEPS FOR PHYSICAL HEALING	135
STEPS FOR SOCIAL HEALING	142

PART FOUR: REBUILDING TRUST — 149

APOLOGY	154
TRUTH	158
HONESTY	160
TRANSPARENCY	161

TIME	163
TALKING	164
TRANSFORMATION	165
HUMILITY	166
HONOR	169
PATIENCE	170
RELIABILITY	172
AFFIRMATION	174
ACCENTUATE POSITIVE EXPERIENCES	175
ACKNOWLEDGE EMOTIONS YOU ARE PROCESSING	176
ADDRESS TRIGGERS	176
AVOID CONTINUAL SURVEILLANCE	177
AVOID IMPLEMENTING RIGID RULES	177
TAKE TIME TO CONNECT	178
PRACTICAL DEMONSTRATIONS OF REBUILDING TRUST	179
TAKE TIME FOR PERSONAL GROWTH	179

NOTES 185

I dedicate this book to my lovely wife, Beverly. We have recently celebrated our 50th wedding anniversary, and throughout these many years, she has been very supportive of me in the ministry. Her love, laughter, sacrifices, and commitment over these years have never gone unnoticed or unappreciated. In addition, I dedicate this book to my two sons, Tommy and Timothy, my two daughter-in-law's, Christa and Yalexa, and my three lovely Grandchildren, CJ, Abygail, and Zayden.

FOREWORD

Tom Twigg joined our pastoral staff at Faith Church, Summerville, SC, in October 2023, and what a wonderful addition he has been. He has incredible integrity and many faithful years of Pastoral experience. He serves our team in Pastoral Care and Counseling. He has journeyed with our people through grief, sickness, separation, addictive behaviors, and a host of other crises.

His book, Crushed, is a must-read for counselors, pastors, and anyone who has experienced the heartbreak of infidelity. He has done extensive research and covers every emotion that a couple goes through. More importantly, his book brings hope and healing to broken couples. His personal counseling, research, and Biblical knowledge come together in this book, Crushed. This book will be a staple in my library to help wounded couples in the future. It is good to know that through Christ Jesus, there is forgiveness and hope for a wonderful future!

Larry Burgbacher
Lead Pastor, Faith Church, Summerville, SC

INTRO

CRUSHED

Sally and Jeff came to my office, and as Sally sat down, I immediately knew something was wrong as the tears streamed down her face. About a year ago, she and her husband had been in my office for counseling to address Jeff's drug addiction. Jeff had made significant progress and had been clean for over a year. Sally had become pregnant with their second child, and both were happy. I assumed the issue was a relapse on Jeff's part, but that wasn't the case. Jeff spoke calmly and admitted he had been sexually unfaithful to his wife. I will never forget the emotional hurt on Sally's face. She felt **CRUSHED.**

Job experienced the emotional loss of all his children, the physical agony of painful boils covering him from head to toe, and the financial devastation of losing seven thousand sheep, three thousand camels, and five hundred yokes of oxen. On top of this, he faced the tormenting words of three friends, and cried out "How long will you torment me and crush me with words" (Job 19:2, NIV)? Negative words can have a devastating impact, and who can bear the weight of the negative words of infidelity without feeling crushed?

Infidelity has been defined in various ways, including sexual, emotional, internet, and pornographic infidelity. Some view it as a violation of the marital covenant relationship through a sexual relationship with a third party. Others see the possibility for emotional infidelity, where a spouse in a committed relationship willingly shares their deepest feelings with someone outside the marriage, breaching trust. Such emotional connections can lead to a greater investment of one's time and finances and may progress to an illicit sexual relationship. Generally, infidelity is viewed as any relationship that secretly, romantically, emotionally, and exclusively violates one's marital relationship.[1] Dr. Linda Mintle described adultery as involving sexual relationships outside of marriage and stated that "infidelity is about dishonesty."[2]

Infidelity shatters the feelings of security that make a spouse feel treasured, valued, and exclusively connected to his or her spouse. When an act of infidelity breaks this physical, emotional, psychological, and spiritual security, overwhelming and destructive emotions arise—fear, anxiety, uncertainty, doubt, distrust, hurt, abandonment, and betrayal. Much like a balloon released after being inflated, spinning uncontrollably through the air, the once safe and secure life now feels like it is spiraling helplessly out of control.

The covenant relationship of unity, continuity, and security has been deeply severed, unleashing an avalanche of emotions—devastation, anger, resentment, woundedness, bitterness, and shame—all tied to this ultimate betrayal. The betrayed spouse is left feeling helplessly **CRUSHED.** Cindy Beall felt crushed. In her book, *Healing Your Marriage When Trust is Broken,* she shared how God had begun healing her heart while she was in Texas, yet she still struggled with the reality that her husband was the father of a baby with another woman. Every time she thought about it, she felt crushed. She wrote, "When I said my wedding vows to my husband and he said his to me, forsaking all others was a part of the deal. I was absolutely on board with that."[3]

It's important to recognize that, while infidelity is often associated with men, women also commit infidelity. Dr. James Dobson, referencing a poll, noted that married women under the age of twenty-nine had significantly more affairs than men in the same age group.

Couples often question if reconciliation is possible as they work to navigate the rift caused by infidelity. Like Sally and Jeff, whom we mentioned earlier, were able to move forward and find reconciliation, you too can find reconciliation. I have known other couples who have survived such a breach, but it required intentional effort to rebuild fragile trust. This process involved repentance, forgiveness, and a strong determination to pursue healing. It also necessitated understanding the contributing factors that led to the affair.

In the journey toward reconciliation, it is important to remember Christ's teaching on sexual infidelity, particularly adultery: divorce is permissible, but it is not mandatory.

Dr. Kathy Nickerson, a relationship expert who has worked with thousands of couples, expressed her sincere belief that a couple's relationship can become "better" after an affair than it was before.[4] In his book *A Celebration of Sex,* Dr. Douglass E. Rosenau offered an inspiring message to those navigating the pain of physical or sexual betrayal. "Most marriages in which both partners are committed to making the partnership work and go through the confession and repentance process usually survive and often become more intimate."[5]

I write this book to encourage you that even after experiencing the pain of destructive betrayal and feeling **CRUSHED,** reconciliation in your marriage is possible. As you sincerely work toward this goal, you can renew your commitment to the sacred marriage covenant you once made to each other in the presence of God and witnesses.

The first part of this book is titled "Dealing with Feelings," where we explore the flood of emotions that rush in when trust is severed in a committed relationship. I've outlined a variety of emotions—some may resonate with you, while others may not. This section comes first, before defining infidelity, because of the intense and explosive power of these feelings. Dr. Archbald Hart and Dr. Sharon May, in their book *Safe Haven Marriage,* stated that "Emotions direct and fuel the way husbands and wives relate to one another."[6] How you handle and express your emotions will shape the trajectory of your marriage after the heartbreaking discovery of betrayal.

The discovery of infidelity may trigger emotions that feel as wild and uncontrollable as a mustang. It's essential to separate the discovery of infidelity from the recovery process. Questions arise: Is the relationship repairable? Is it salvageable? How is it possible to move forward, and what will moving forward look like? In addition, the emotional instability triggered by infidelity can put the faithful spouse at risk. Therefore, it is crucial to identify and understand the emotions being navigated.

In the second part of the book *Defining Infidelity,* we work toward a shared understanding of what infidelity entails, exploring different types of affairs, including emotional affairs, physical/sexual affairs, pornography (silent infidelity), cybersex, friends-with-benefits, and sexting. In the third part of the book, *Dealing with Healing*, we look at some practical steps for emotional, physical, psychological, and spiritual healing from the painful betrayal of infidelity.

In the last part of the book, we address *Rebuilding Trust*. This section is the culmination of all the previous parts and addresses what hurting couples long to achieve most. Rebuilding trust provides hope amid uncertainty, light amid the darkness, peace amid fear, strength amid weakness, security amid shame, courage amid fear, calm amid provocation, love amid hate, sweetness amid bitterness, cheerfulness amid depression, joy amid despair, faith amid unbelief, self-worth amid embarrassment, and calm amid anxiety.

This kind of trust is not beyond your reach—it is within your grasp. Though it demands sincere sacrifice and commitment, it offers the promise of a new beginning and a continual expectancy of happiness.

PART 1

DEALING WITH FEELINGS

"Feelings are something you have, not something you are."

–SHANNON L. ADLER

It is vitally important to recognize, identify, and express our feelings. During the discovery of infidelity, it is natural for feelings to intensify, but a spouse must be careful not to allow feelings to dominate logical thinking. At times, this will be very difficult because, as human beings, we were created to experience emotions, and navigating infidelity can feel like being on an emotional roller coaster. There is always the challenge not to allow our feelings to dominate our decision-making.

However, on the flip side, along with our intellect and will, God uses feelings as an avenue to communicate with us. We should not deny our emotions, as they are part of how we are created in the image of God—who possesses intellect, will, and emotions that are pure, genuine, and untainted by sin.

Our soul is comprised of our intellect, will, and emotions. In His wisdom, God gave human beings the distinct ability to experience and express all kinds of emotions. The word *emotion* finds its origin in the Latin word *emovare,* which means "to move." Hence, emotions are commonly understood to be feelings. Three words are often used to describe different aspects of our emotions: affect, passion, and mood.

Affect references both our conscious and unconscious feelings. *Passion* describes intense emotions, and when we use the word *mood*, we are talking about emotions that have a longer duration.[7]

Some emotions are more noticeable than others, and the intensity of these feelings can differ greatly between spouses. Some new emotions may also begin to manifest themselves as you process the painful reality of betrayal.

Understanding your emotions may challenge you to consider a provocative thought by Jeanne Allen in her book entitled *Untangle Your Emotions,* where she firmly expresses, "...Emotions are not meant to control us, they are meant to inform us."[8] What are your emotions trying to tell you about yourself? How are they helping you to express what you are truly feeling?

It is important to express your feelings. While a spouse may attempt to hide or mask their emotions, this approach is not healthy. When feelings are bottled up, we become like a colander— our emotions, like water, inevitably find a way to escape. They often surface through the tone of our words, our attitude, or our body language. A hurting spouse may insist, "I said, I am fine," but their tone and body language often speak volumes louder than their words.

In our desire for emotional health, we must recognize that we are human beings with feelings. Peter Scazzero highlighted the necessity of acknowledging our emotions when he wrote, "To minimize or deny what we feel is a distortion of what it means to be image bearers of God. To the degree that we are unable to express our emotions, we remain impaired in our ability to love God, others, and ourselves well."[9] Don't shy away from your feelings or deny them; instead, express them to God, a trusted friend, a counselor, or a therapist.

Dr. James Dobson stated that when emotions are "forced to stand alone our feelings usually reveal themselves to be unreliable and ephemeral and even a bit foolish." Therefore, we must endeavor to find a balance—avoiding the extremes of ignoring our feelings or allowing them to overrule us.

The following list of emotions is not exhaustive, but it includes some that you may identify with and find yourself desperately struggling to navigate after discovering your spouse's infidelity. Alongside each emotion, I have included thoughts that may help you address and work through the predominant feelings you are experiencing.

But before identifying these emotions, it is important to understand how men and women differ in their perspectives and experiences of sexual infidelity.

Dr. Pierce J. Howard, writing about affairs, pointed out, "There are two aspects of extramarital affairs: the sex act itself and the emotional attachment to another person. Women tend to experience more distress over emotional attachment than to the act itself; the opposite is true of men."[10] He also noted key differences in how men respond to jealousy. Men often display jealousy when they discover their wife had sexual intercourse with another man, regardless of how serious the relationship was or how long it lasted. Women, on the other hand, are typically less concerned that their men had a one-night stand but feel more threatened by a competing relationship that could result in the loss of financial resources.[11]

I am not minimizing the deep emotional pain both spouses experience, but I am simply pointing out how men and women differ in their responses.

ANGER

Gary Chapman stated, "Although we normally think of anger as an emotion, it is in reality a cluster of emotions involving the body, the mind, and the will."[12] A survey revealed four common triggers for anger, "a love of control, a desire for possession, the high value we place on sexual intimacy, and the proud treasure of our reputation."[13] Dr. James Dobson identified four causes of angry feelings: a response to frustration, fatigue, embarrassment, and rejection.[14] In most cases of infidelity, anger seems to dominate.

Mike came into my office and shared his story. When he discovered his wife was sexually involved with another man, he was overwhelmed with anger. He admitted that in his rage, he took a bottle of wine and a shotgun, placed them in his truck, and headed to a party where his wife and lover were present. He planned to shoot them.

On the way, Mike received a phone call from his father-in-law, who asked about his whereabouts and intentions.

He told Mike that his daughter and her lover had left the party and urged him to travel to his home and talk. His father-in-law persuaded him to cool off and recognize the criminal implications of his planned actions. In this situation, his father-in-law helped Mike see that his decisions should be guided by sound logic rather than emotions.

The Apostle Paul encouraged Christians "to be angry and sin not" (Ephesians 4:26, KJV). It is doubtful that a spouse would not experience anger upon discovering the crushing truth of infidelity. Anger is perhaps one of the first emotions one feels and must be addressed. This is likely first because it is our first instinct—our built-in desire to avoid emotional hurt. As a defensive mechanism, anger often becomes the immediate reaction to the discovery of sexual infidelity. When Paul urged individuals to be angry and not sin, his exhortation carried three implications.

1. He was implying that no one should ignore the fact that he or she is angry.
2. Each person may voice the anger he or she feels. Gary Chapman wisely commented on the need for a person to express their anger, stating, "Unexpressed anger produces death like a malignant cancerous tumor slowly destroying life's fiber."[15] However, a person must be careful to express their anger to their spouse in a healthy

manner, as their anger will subside, but damaging words can remain forever in the heart and mind of a spouse. Solomon declared, "Reckless words pierce like a sword, but the tongue of the wise brings healing" (Proverbs 12:1, NIV).
3. Each person is responsible for his or her actions. Solomon stated, "Fools give full vent to their rage, but the wise bring calm in the end" (Proverbs 29:11, NIV). We will either rule over our anger or be ruled by it; we will either take control of anger or be controlled by it.

Have you ever witnessed the destruction caused by a tornado, where everything in its path is destroyed? That's what uncontrolled anger does. It can lead to one being controlled by legal authorities and add further emotional trauma to an already difficult situation. Taking control of one's anger can prevent actions or words that will later be regretted. Self-control may begin by walking away from the situation and giving yourself time to calm down. Controlling anger also prevents a spouse from justifying their wrong actions. "You cannot see your reflection in boiling water. Similarly, you cannot see the truth in a state of anger."[16]

Anger can be a healthy emotion for the spouse who has suffered the pain of infidelity. You might ask, "How is this possible?" Anger may be healthy because it demonstrates that you care. The acronym *C.A.R. E.* captures the healthy aspect of anger.

C – Concern:

Anger shows that you are concerned about your marriage. When you said your vows before God and witnesses, you were unconditionally committing yourself to one another, and those vows held deep meaning for you. Instead of building a wall with vitriolic words, you are focused on building, if possible, a bridge of reconciliation.

A - Articulation:

Anger allows you to articulate what you are feeling. By expressing your anger, you acknowledge that an offense has taken place. Healthy articulation prevents you from repressing your emotions and helps you constructively process your anger. By voicing your anger, you can avoid letting bitterness take root.

R - Responsibility.

You and your spouse each contribute to the relational dynamic in your marriage. Every marriage has a unique dynamic because each person brings their personality, morality, and rationality into the relationship. When infidelity occurs, both the betrayed and the betrayer are responsible for the relational dynamic that exists in the marriage. However, the betrayed spouse must recognize the betraying spouse as solely responsible for the act of infidelity. The innocent party is not at fault and must refuse to allow the betraying partner to shift or transfer blame for their wrongdoing. The betrayed spouse must not accept responsibility for the betrayer's wrong choice in committing infidelity.

It is essential to understand and acknowledge that, regardless of any shortcomings in the life of the betrayed spouse, the spouse who committed sexual infidelity made deliberate choices that led to the act of infidelity. The innocent spouse must be aware of the danger of self-blame, which is often based on false perceptions of their inadequacies. While the betrayed spouse may think of "a thousand things" they could have done better in the relationship, none of those things would diminish or alter the betraying spouse's responsibility for their choices.

E - Expressing

Expressing your anger to your spouse is healthy, as opposed to unhealthily repressing it. It allows you to address your anger instead of acting out in aggression. A wounded spouse may find it beneficial to express their anger to a trusted friend. However, it is never healthy to respond to an offense with vengeance. Subotnik and Harris emphasized the importance of expressing anger constructively, describing it as a balance between suppressing anger and expressing unrestrained anger. They viewed constructive anger as moderate and directed at the right target— your offending spouse. [17]

It may also be healthy and wise to seek the guidance of a marriage counselor or pastor to help process feelings of anger. The goal is not to prolong anger but to process it, voicing emotions in a way that avoids vengeance or violence. Solomon offers a powerful illustration of this truth: "Where there is no wood the fire goes out..." (Proverbs 26:20, NKJV).

A hurting spouse must carefully consider how anger may turn into destructive anger. While anger might harm the offending spouse, it is far more likely to harm the innocent party if they do not ask the Lord to forgive the offending spouse. As the saying goes, "Unforgiveness is like drinking poison and waiting for the offending person to die."

JEALOUSY

Jealousy is as old as humanity, as seen in the story of Cain and Able (Genesis 4). Jealousy can manifest as both healthy and unhealthy, fostering either protective care and concern or destructive acts that, in extreme cases, may lead to murder. "Opinions vary as to whether there is a cohesive continuum connecting 'normal' jealousy with the extreme instance of morbid or delusional jealousy."[18] Dr. Pierce J. Howard described jealousy as "a condition in which all the major negative emotions are activated: fear, anger, depression, disgust, etc."[19]

Over the years, I have encountered cases of men, driven by morbid jealousy (sometimes referred to as pathological jealousy), committing murder over a girlfriend or wife—or even killing their girlfriend or wife. In some tragic instances, jealousy or depression may sadly influence a person to attempt or complete suicide. As William Penn declared, "The jealous are troublesome to others but a torment to themselves."[20]

Research has revealed that men and women react differently to jealousy. Men tend to be more jealous of physical infidelity, while women are more jealous of emotional infidelity.[21] In both scenarios, whether the infidelity is physical or emotional, another person is intruding upon a cherished connection. This justified jealousy can lead to emotional anger, which must be handled healthily and constructively.

BITTERNESS

Have you ever climbed a spiral staircase? You move around and around, steadily heading to a specific destination. Bitterness is the final step in a spiraling journey of emotions—resentment, disappointment, sadness, anger, and feeling unappreciated, devalued, or disrespected.

Bitterness doesn't suddenly appear; it is the result of a cumulative process of dwelling on these emotions. You don't go to bed feeling happy and content and wake up bitter the next morning.

If you are navigating the pain of infidelity, you must guard your heart against the poison of bitterness. Paul admonished Simon from Samaria to repent of his wickedness, saying, "For I see that you are poisoned by bitterness and bound by iniquity" (Acts 8:23). Martin Luther King Jr. also recognized the danger of bitterness and wisely counseled, "Never succumb to the temptation of bitterness."[22]

DEPRESSION

The feeling of depression is easily recognized through emotions such as feeling downcast, gloomy, inadequate, lonely, or sad. Other signs that may accompany these feelings include "decreased energy, fluctuating body weight, depleted concentration, bouts of crying, hopelessness or despair, a disinterest in pleasurable activities, social withdrawal and thoughts of suicide"[23].

As human beings, we all experience mild depression that may last a few minutes or a few days. Emotional highs and lows are a natural part of life. However, when this depression persists for weeks or months, it may indicate clinical depression, a condition that psychiatrists identify as requiring professional help.

Shirley Glass stated that when she began therapy sessions addressing infidelity, wives were more anxious and depressed than men. She revealed that "32 percent of unfaithful wives were severely anxious compared with 10 percent of unfaithful husbands; 27 percent of unfaithful wives and 14 percent of unfaithful husbands were clinically depressed."[24]

In the United States, hospitalization due to mental illnesses, such as depression, accounts for one-third of the most common causes for admittance, particularly affecting individuals aged 18 to 44.[25]

A sense of loss often triggers depression, and the greater the loss, the greater the depression. For example, in the book of Job, we see that Job suffered profound losses, which led him to feel depressed and curse the day he was born (Job 3:1). Depression may also result from "repressing or denying appropriate feelings of anger".[26]

Elijah, a man of great faith, also experienced a bout of depression while reflecting on the faithfulness of Israel's leaders. In his despair, he wished he could die (I Kings 19-3-4). Like Elijah, we sometimes reach an emotional and physical breaking point where we cry out, "It is enough" (I Kings 19:4, NKJV).

This point of despair often manifests when the harsh reality of forfeited trust sets in. Additionally, you may be experiencing the crushing effects of loss—the loss of your soul mate, your home, financial security, transportation, friends, health, peace, happiness, and even the dream you and your spouse once shared.

When depression stretches out its unwelcoming arm and seizes you in its grip, leaving you feeling alone, disconnected, meaningless, worthless, and insignificant—when you lack both the motivation and energy to move forward—turn to your kind heavenly Father and inquire about the steps you can take. As a child of God, you have the great privilege of sharing your thoughts and feelings with Him. Peter reminded his readers that God cares about their cares (I Peter 5:7). David declared, "I took my troubles to the Lord; I cried out to him, and he answered me" (Psalm 120:1, NIV).

HOPELESSNESS

Hopelessness, like a devouring lion, can consume you. This is particularly true when someone discovers infidelity. A wife may entertain the thought that her husband was unfaithful because she was not enough. Similarly, a husband may believe he was not enough for his wife.

Alternatively, a spouse may accept the shifting of blame, believing their partner acted out because they were not providing enough sex.

Dr. Kevin Skinner observed that when women accept such beliefs as truth, it often leads to an increase in depression and anxiety. He further noted that these feelings intensify when a woman begins to view herself as not enough, a failure, or flawed, leaving her feeling helpless to fix the situation.[27]

You may have falsely assumed that reconciliation in your marriage is impossible, and this sense of hopelessness may lead to depression. During these times, you can look to Jesus for peace, hope, and rest in His unchanging love, mercy, goodness, kindness, and grace.

Amid the despair, there is good news. Reconciliation is always a possibility when there is sincere repentance and when both spouses are committed to working on saving their marriage. This may involve seeking professional counseling, attending groups that deal with sexual addiction, and participating in marriage seminars.

When David experienced depression, he questioned his feelings and redirected his thoughts toward God. He said, "Why art thou cast down, O my soul? And why art thou disquieted within me? Hope thou in God; For I shall yet praise him, who is the health of my countenance and my God" (Psalm 42:11, KJV).

God's love is stronger than the depression or hopelessness you may be navigating. There are times when we must trust God, even when we cannot understand His providential workings in our lives. When Jacob was overwhelmed by the demands placed on him, he cried out in agony, "Everything is against me" (Genesis 42:36, NIV). Yet, the fuller picture revealed that God was making provisions for his future. Jacob and his family would migrate to the land of Egypt, where God would raise the nation of Israel, from whom the Messiah would come.

GUILT

James Dobson defined guilt as arising from a violation of our inner code of conduct and acknowledged that, for some people, this sense of disapproval can be fragile, allowing it to be ignored or seared.[28]

The guilt associated with infidelity may be experienced by one or both spouses. The innocent spouse may question what they did wrong and may even blame themselves for the infidelity.

The cheater may feel the crushing weight of guilt for being unfaithful to their spouse and betraying their deep moral values. They may wrestle with thoughts of how they could have made a different choice and walked away from the sexual act. Whatever thoughts arise, the wounded and innocent spouse must realize that infidelity was a deliberate choice made by their spouse.

Not all guilt is harmful. James Dobson recognized that feelings of disapproval can serve as a powerful motivator for responsible behavior.[29] When we transition from perceived irresponsible behavior to perceived responsible behavior, the disapproval (or conviction) for our actions becomes a guiding force, directing us toward the right moral path—especially when our moral conduct is grounded in the clear commandments of God and the conviction of the Holy Spirit.

There is a clear difference between shame and guilt. Guilt declares, "I did something bad," while shame shouts, "I am bad." Shirley Glass explained that guilt can exist even if no one else is aware of the transgression, whereas shame arises in response to external consequences—when one is caught doing something wrong.[30] In other words, it's like being caught with your hand in the cookie jar. Heather Daveduik Gingrich in her book, *Restoring the Shattered Self*, references S.H. Martin (1990), who observed, "Guilt is more a response to doing, while shame is a response to being."[31]

David undoubtedly struggled with the guilt of infidelity, and we can learn much from him about processing guilt. His prayer reflects the need for spiritual renewal in the heart of a cheating spouse. This renewal is revealed as David prays, "Create in me a pure heart, O God, and renew a steadfast spirit with me. Do not cast me from your presence or take your Holy Spirit from me. Restore to me the joy of your salvation and grant me a willing spirit to sustain me" (Psalm 51:10-12, NIV).

A spiritual renewal begins with forgiving oneself. While there is never justification or rationalization for committing infidelity, there is also no justification for carrying the crushing weight of guilt indefinitely when God promises, "If we confess our sins, He is just and faithful to cleanse us from all unrighteousness" (I John 1:9). In our brokenness and confession of sin, we find true freedom. Guilt serves no purpose when we have sincerely repented and confessed our sins to Christ.

Satan seeks to make guilt a permanent companion, following us throughout the years. Paul certainly provided the remedy for this nagging guilt, which leads to endless self-condemnation, when he penned these words, "There is therefore now no condemnation to them which are in Christ Jesus, who walk not after the flesh but after the Spirit" (Romans 8:1, KJV).

BLAME

"...Women are more prone than men to blame themselves for their partner's infidelity."[32] Whether a man or woman, the list of "What Ifs" often surfaces, leading one to suppose that taking a different course of action could have prevented the infidelity. When a person assumes sole responsibility for the blame, they effectively exonerate their spouse from their responsibility for the infidelity.

Marriages are comprised of two individuals, both of whom have entered into a covenant agreement to remain exclusively committed to one another. Any violation of that agreement highlights the irresponsibility of the offending party and cannot be absorbed by the innocent party; to do so would be ludicrous. A man or woman cannot prevent their spouse from choosing to engage in sexual infidelity. While every marriage faces challenges and complex circumstances, these never excuse the actions of the offending party.

HURT

The words of sexual infidelity are often verbalized as, "I cheated on you." Upon hearing these words, a spouse immediately experiences a flood of negative emotions. Counselors frequently hear the heart-wrenching phrase,

"It hurts so much," spoken through tears as the counselee struggles to convey the depth of their emotional wound.

Just as some physical wounds heal quickly while others take a long time, depending on their severity, the emotional wound caused by a broken marriage covenant resembles a serious wound—it takes a long time to heal and leaves a psychological scar. Amanda Aliff stated, "Trauma can be anything that is difficult for a person to process."[33] She proceeded to say, "Infidelity is multi-layered and is considered betrayal trauma."[34] Is there any wonder why "It hurts so much"?

Healing from the trauma of betrayal is a difficult process, and the timeline will vary for each individual. The deeper the wound, the longer the healing journey. Injurious statements like "I told you I was sorry" or "Just get over it" demonstrate a lack of understanding of the depth of hurt the wounded spouse is experiencing and underscore the desperate need for a proper healing process.

Some therapists today refer to the emotional impact of infidelity as PISD (Post Infidelity Stress Disorder). Unlike PTSD (Post Traumatic Stress Disorder), which can result from a range of traumatic experiences, PISD is a psychological disorder triggered by infidelity. Based on a study in 2021, PISD may affect 30% to 60% of people experiencing the pain of infidelity.[35]

DISBELIEF

The severity of the discovery of infidelity is influenced by various factors: the strengths of the marriage, the emotional relationship, the existing intimacy, the social stability, one's perception of the relationship, verbal expressions of love, the longevity of the marriage, and the life you and your spouse have built together. As tears stream down your cheeks, you question, "How could this ever happen to me?" You struggle to find words to express the sudden reality of infidelity as tears of unbelief continue to flow. Acknowledging your loss, going through the grieving process, and seeking counseling can help guide you toward emotional stability.

Perhaps the greatest action you can take when your world has turned upside down in an instant is to talk to God. Share with Him your anger, sorrow, sadness, dismay, or disbelief. David wrote, "In my distress, I cried unto the Lord, and He heard me and delivered me from all my fears" (Psalm 120: 1). You may not have an answer to your "Why," but you do have the solution to the situation. The solution is to trust in the unimpeachable integrity of God, who will work on your behalf and never leave or forsake you.

DISGUST

Webster defines "disgust," when used as a verb, as "to provoke loathing, repugnance or aversion; be offensive to; to cause (one) to lose an interest or intention."[36] Disgust is not usually one of the prominent emotions verbalized by the offended party, but it often emerges following the discovery of physical or sexual infidelity. The offended spouse may express this disgust with statements such as, "You make me sick to my stomach, and I can't stand to look at you," or "When I think of you being in bed with another person, I want to vomit."

A riveting and traumatic story in 2 Samuel 13 reveals the depth of perversion that lust, masquerading as love, can reach, and the devastating emotional words of hate and disgust that can flow from a nefarious and hardened heart.

The story unfolds with Ammon, the crown prince of King David and the firstborn of his wife Ahinoam (II Samuel 3:2). Ammon became lovesick with Tamar, the sister of Absalom, both children of David's wife Talmai (II Samuel 3:3). Tamar was a virgin—a young woman available for marriage—but she was off-limits to Ammon because marriage between half-siblings was forbidden. Ammon was so tormented by his desire for what he could not possess. Day by day, he grew more and more obsessed with her beauty, to the point of losing both his sleep and appetite, making himself physically ill over her.

Jonadab, Ammon's cousin and friend, noticed his haggard appearance and questioned him about it. Ammon confessed that he was in love with his brother Absalom's sister, Tamar. Jonadab contrived a plan, urging Ammon to lie down and pretend to be ill. When his father David inquired about his so-called illness, Ammon was to answer, "Let my sister Tamar come and give me bread to eat and prepare food in my sight, that I may see it and eat it from her hand" (II Samuel 13:5, ESV).

Amnon listened to Jonadab. David was persuaded and instructed Tamar to go to Ammon's house, and Tamar obeyed as she was directed. Ammon refused to eat the food she had prepared in the presence of others in the house. He commanded everyone to leave and then asked Tamar to bring the food to his chamber. When she entered his chamber and presented the food to him, Ammon seized her hand and asked her to lie down with him. She refused, viewing such a sexual act as outrageous, and knowing it would result in her shame and folly for Ammon. But Ammon would not listen to her. He overpowered and sexually violated her.

Take note of the words found in 2 Samuel 13:15, "Then Ammon hated her with very great hatred; so that the hatred with which he hated her was greater than the love with which he had loved her." His visible actions punctuated his vitriolic words as he threw Tamar out of his house and bolted the door.

Such words and actions continue to occur in the 21st century. The innocent spouse, once cherished, learns the painful news of physical or sexual betrayal and often responds to the guilty spouse with words of disgust and rejection. In some cases, the innocent spouse experiences the unwarranted disdain and disgust of the guilty party as he or she exits the home.

SHAME

Shame is a powerful and painful emotion, one that all human beings have experienced at some point in their lives. It is of great importance to recognize that shame may stem from either our own choices (actions) or the choices (actions) of others. Put another way, shame may result from our failures or the failure of others that have consequences in our lives. For example, a spouse who is innocent of sexual betrayal may still bear the shame of their partner's actions when the infidelity is discovered by family members or those in the community.

Steven Tracy defined shame as "a deep, painful sense of inadequacy and personal failure based on the inability to live up to a standard of conduct."[37]

In his definition of shame, Edward Welch declared, "Shame is the deep sense that you are unacceptable because of something you did, something done to you, or something associated with you. You feel exposed and humiliated."[38] Curt Thompson noted that shame "may be obscured in the language of other emotions we are more familiar with such as sadness, anger, disappointment or even guilt."[39]

Dr. Kathy Nickerson quoted Brene Brown who provided the following perspective on guilt and shame:

> I believe that guilt is adaptive and helpful—it's holding something we've done or failed to do up against our values and feelings psychological discomfort. I define shame as the intensely painful feeling or experience of believing that we are flawed and therefore unworthy of love and belonging—something we've experienced, done, or failed to do makes us unworthy of connection. I don't believe shame is helpful or productive. In fact, I think shame is much more likely to be the source of destructive, hurtful behavior than the solution or cure. I think the fear of connection can make us dangerous. Nickerson, 202, 203-204[40]

When it comes to infidelity, the guilty partner is often deeply aware of the feeling of shame, which, like a blue crab, latches on to its food source and refuses to let go. "Shame attaches to our hearts and taints our most significant relational longings, desires, needs, hopes and wants with self-doubt critical judgment and insecurity."[41]

The faithful partner often carries shame, subjectively feeling that they are not man or woman enough for their spouse or that something is physically, emotionally, or mentally wrong with them. Perhaps a man may feel he is not handsome enough, while a woman may feel she is not beautiful enough for their spouse.

While counseling individuals guilty of physical or sexual infidelity who feel an element of shame, it is not unusual to discover that infidelity may have occurred several times in the marriage. This indicates that shame, though significant and real, does not necessarily prevent the guilty spouse from repeated offenses.

David felt both guilt and shame when his sexual infidelity with Bathsheba was exposed. However, he took full responsibility for his actions, and we never see David committing the same sin with another man's wife. Shame can serve as a deterrent to immoral actions if it is accompanied by accountability, responsibility, and sincere contrition.

Simon Peter used a lion as a metaphor for Satan. When Satan roars "S H A M E," provoking you to feel disgusted with yourself, or seditiously whispers suggestive destructive thoughts, it is crucial to remember your identity in Christ.

When God created Adam and Eve, He placed them in the Garden of Eden with the foremost purpose of worshiping Him. Satan entered the garden and "successfully sabotaged" their spiritual and moral identity.[42]

When Satan diligently works to blind your eyes and prevent you from discovering and embracing your spiritual and moral identity, let me remind you of who you are in Christ. You are a child of God (Galatians 3:26). You are created in the image of God (Genesis 1:27). You are God's temple (I Corinthians 3:16). You are fearfully and wonderfully made (Psalm 139:14). You are a new creature in Christ (2 Corinthians 5:17). You are being transformed into Christlikeness (2 Corinthians 3:18). You are God's workmanship (Ephesians 2:10). Christ died for you (Romans 5:8). God loves you (John 3:16, I John 4:10). Nothing can separate you from the love of God that is in Christ Jesus (Romans 8:38-39).

This process of becoming who you are in Christ Jesus is not instantaneous. However, the Holy Spirit empowers us to live out our identity in Him. Dutch Sheets wrote, "We must learn how to take hold by faith and implement the biblical principles that govern the receiving of what He says is already ours. Then we can become who we are and receive all He promised."[43]

EMBARRASSMENT

Both a husband and wife may experience embarrassment when the truth of physical, sexual, or emotional fidelity is exposed to the public, friends, or family members. The primary aspect of embarrassment is that the innocent spouse often views the guilty spouse's moral failure as a reflection of themselves. The oft-repeated phrase flows from their lips, "What will people think?"

The innocent spouse may develop a fearful perception that all eyes of the community, close friends, or relatives are watching and judging them. This leads to the fear that they will be seen as less important or valued in the social world. The guilty spouse may also express the same thoughts.

This is a heavy and self-conscious thought, made even more difficult to bear in today's world where there is the prominence of social media. However, the reality is that not everyone in the community is judging or acting in such a way. An innocent spouse can find great profit in realizing that reputation is what people think you are, but character is who you truly are—even in the dark when no one is watching.

Martin Luther is quoted as saying, "You cannot keep birds from flying over your head, but you can keep them from building a nest in your hair."

Samuel stated, "The Lord does not look at things people look at, People look at the outward appearance, but the Lord looks at the heart" (I Samuel 16.7, NIV). The Lord perfectly knows all the facts and the sincerity of the heart. If the guilty spouse sincerely repents of their moral failure, the Lord hears their humble cry and forgives.

It is also comforting for the offending spouse to acknowledge that all humanity shares a sinful nature, and none is innocent of transgressing moral law. Saint Paul declared, "For all have sinned and fall short of the glory of God" (Romans 3:23, KJV).

FEAR

"Fear is a physical and emotional response to a perceived threat or danger."[44]

Fear has an uncanny ability to substantiate its existence, interrupt reason, and paralyze our will. The faithful spouse may wrestle with fear, finding it extremely difficult to trust their spouse again. They may fallaciously reason, "If my spouse has been unfaithful once, I fear he or she will be unfaithful again." The trust that has been violated now feels fragile and even more untenable.

The sudden disclosure of infidelity creates a seven-lane expressway for multiple fears. For example, a mom with young children may ask herself, "How am I going to make it financially? How am I going to pay the rent? If I can't pay the rent, where will the children and I live? Who's going to be home with our children when I go to work? Who will see them off to school? How will the children react when they realize their daddy isn't coming home? How will this affect my children emotionally, psychologically, socially, spiritually, and financially?"

A wife may be fearful in the middle of the night when she hears unidentifiable sounds. Similarly, a husband abandoned by an adulterous wife may worry about how he will manage on a single income and fear losing the house. Other sociological scenarios raise a multitude of questions germane to the situation, each giving rise to different fears.

As painful as our emotional fears may be, especially the fear of being alone, they can sometimes be a good thing. Think for a minute about what you fear physically. Perhaps, as a little boy or girl, you remember the physical pain of a lit match, a lump of hot coal, or the flame from a gas stove. That experience likely gave you a greater appreciation and respect for fire. You not only learned to respect it but also, in some sense, to fear it because of the pain associated with it.

Those experiencing the emotional pain of infidelity may find fear to be a good friend. The fear of being emotionally burned again in a relationship can serve as a protective mechanism, encouraging you to give yourself the necessary time to heal from your emotional wound. It can also prompt you to establish healthy boundaries and place guardrails in your life, enabling you to trust again. You can become more cautious, and refrain from moving too fast in forming an intimate relationship, all the while expressing realistic expectations.

By identifying and embracing our fears, we can move forward in life without allowing them to paralyze us. Like a turtle retreating into its shell for protection, we assess our vulnerability in forming new relationships. Then, with courage, we slowly stick our heads out again and move forward, one careful step at a time.

ANXIETY

In the United States, anxiety disorder is the most common mental health condition. It is estimated that approximately forty million adults, ages eighteen and older, struggle with this disorder.[45] Anxiety disorder occurs when the emotion of fear becomes a constant companion, bringing with it a suitcase of physical symptoms. Unlike transient fear, anxiety disorder can persist for six months or more.[46]

When we are anxious, our focus shifts from seeking and doing the will of God to concentrating on ourselves. We pivot from an eternal perspective to a temporary one. Instead of focusing on an infinite God, we become consumed with our finite abilities and limitations. In our anxiety, we rush to form our own plans rather than conform to His eternal plan. We substitute His wisdom and understanding with our reasoning.

The difference between fear and anxiety lies in their focus and timing. Fear is an emotional response triggered by a real or perceived imminent threat, while anxiety involves the anticipation of a potential threat that may occur in the future. Fear centers on escape behaviors, such as fight or flight, when one feels an immediate danger. In contrast, anxiety is associated with muscle tension, occurring as one vigilantly prepares for a future danger or cautiously seeks to avoid the perceived threat.[47]

Depression focuses on the past, fear focuses on the present, and anxiety focuses on the future. Max Lucado described fear as seeing a threat and anxiety as imagining a threat.[48] This imagination is often expressed by two little words, "what if". People experiencing anxiety often carry a large basket full of "what ifs." But what if you turned your "what if" into "if when?"

A powerful example of this can be found in the book of Habakkuk. He stated, "Though the fig tree should not blossom, nor fruit be on the vines, the produce of the olive fail and the fields yield no food, the flocks be cut off from the folds and there be no herd in the stalls, yet I will rejoice in the Lord. I will take you in the God of my salvation. God, the Lord, is my strength; He makes my feet like the deer's, He makes me tread on my high places" (Habakkuk 3:17-19, ESV).

We could say, "if when" there are no figs on the tree, "if when" there is no fruit on the vines, "if when" there are no olives on the trees and the olive oil fails, "if when" there are no sheep in the pen, "if when" there are no cattle in the stalls, "I will rejoice in the Lord, and God will be my strength. God will be my provider."

Whatever emotional experience you are navigating, you can further declare: "God will be my healer, God will be my song in the night, God will be my shield and defender, God will be my guide, God will be my shepherd and lead me, God will my counselor and God will be my deliverer!"

When infidelity is discovered and the once peaceful terrain of your heart is invaded by anxiety, you do not have to be controlled by it. Daniel, the prophet in the Old Testament and a man of impeachable integrity, understood the futility of trying to control the future or allowing it to control him. When his enemies conspired against him, and the king ordered him to be placed in a lion's den overnight, he joyfully proclaimed the next morning, "My God sent His angel and shut the lion's mouth, so they have not hurt me…" (Daniel 6:22, NKJV). What was the source of Daniel's strength? It was his faith and trust in the Lord.

The Apostle Paul encouraged the church of Phillippi to avoid the weight of anxiety and offered a remedy for it. "Be anxious for nothing but in everything by prayer and supplication, with thanksgiving, let your requests be known to God" (Philippians 4:6, KJV). It is also interesting to note the previous verse, "Let your gentle spirit be known unto all people. The Lord is near" (Philippians 4:5, KJV). Scholars debate whether the phrase "The Lord is near," should conclude verse 5 or introduce verse 6.

What should not be overlooked is the profound truth that our gentleness should be evident to all, even in the face of suffering or opposition. This characteristic can be cultivated by focusing on the Lord's presence with us. Alternatively, the statement "The Lord is near" can remind us not to be anxious because of His constant presence. In either case, the focus remains on the awesome omnipresence of God that surrounds us.

David, king of Israel, recognized how the consolation of God could change the dynamics of anxiety. He wrote, "When anxiety was great within me, your consolation brought me joy" (Psalm 94:19, NIV).

> Said the robin to the sparrow
> "Friend, I would like to know,
> why do these human beings rush
> about and worry so?"
> Said the sparrow to the robin,

> "Friend, I think it must be
> that they have thy have no
> Heavenly Father
> such as cares for you and me."
> AUTHOR UNKNOWN

PANIC

According to Merriam-Webster, panic is defined as a sudden, overpowering fright or acute, extreme anxiety. It can also refer to a sudden, unreasoning terror often accompanied by mass flight.[49] When you suddenly discover your spouse's infidelity and begin thinking about the imminent sociological, financial, and domestic changes that will take place in your life, you may begin to panic.

Approximately 25% of people in America will experience an anxiety disorder at least once in their lifetime.[50] This can be such a debilitating experience, especially if it leads to significant panic attacks, which are often accompanied by dizziness, a racing heart, hyperventilation, and chest pains.[51]

The sure and solid cure for panic is to lift our eyes to God in prayer and discover that no matter where we are and what we are going through, there is an omnipresent God *with* us every moment of the day. If we will but employ our hearts and efforts in acknowledging such truth, we will, like Jacob of old, discover, "Surely the Lord was in this place was in this place and I knew it not" (Genesis 28:16).

It is important to understand that not everyone is on the same spiritual or psychological plane. In severe cases of panic, where worry has overtaken an individual to the point that they cannot function, they should seek evaluation by a doctor or psychiatrist. If necessary, medication can be an important aid in helping them. The individual should not feel any condemnation for seeking such help.

In her book entitled, *Letting Go of Worry,* Dr. Linda Mintle, a Christian licensed clinical social worker who holds her PhD in urban health and clinical psychology wrote, "Once a level of control is found that allows a person to work in therapy, the person can eventually discontinue the medication. This is especially true when treating panic attacks and phobias."[52]

LONELINESS

Perhaps the most recurring emotion a wounded spouse experiences after separation or divorce is the awful feeling of loneliness. Those who experience emotional pain from sexual betrayal often go through periods of loneliness because of their temporary inability to conquer their fear of trust. This loneliness persists as long as they continue to avoid the possibility of being hurt again in a relationship.

Mary Sarton, in her book *Journal of a Solitude*, wrote, "Loneliness is the poverty of self; solitude is the richness of self."[53] Loneliness, from an emotional aspect, can be deeply uncomfortable and upsetting, whereas being alone may be comfortable and peaceful—at least for a short time. "Loneliness is the state of distress or discomfort that results when one perceives a gap between one's desires for social connection and actual experiences of it."[54]

Lysa Terkeurst, from a very pragmatic point of view, stated that "Alone doesn't just happen when there's no one around. Sometimes *alone* means you're carrying the weight of something hard by yourself. People around you are supportive. But they can't understand the full gravity of what it feels like to you."[55]

Dr. James Dobson observed that a spouse rejected or tossed aside for another intruding lover often expresses that their most painful experience is their loneliness. Such pain is intensified by "knowing that their unfaithful partner is comforted in the embrace of another."[56] You may be experiencing such painful loneliness. Let me exhort you to reach out to a friend or counselor. Be cautious, as loneliness can sometimes drive individuals prematurely into new but unhealthy relationships.

On the positive side, such loneliness resulting from an irreconcilable marriage, after sufficient time and healing, may eventually lead a person into a healthy relationship. The painful lessons learned can become a platform of future health, hope, and happiness.

The television *Alone Series* portrays individuals strategically placed in specific geographical locations with limited survival equipment. Each participant is separated and placed alone at a designated site, and the one who lasts the longest wins a half-million dollars. While they face challenges such as securing food, water, fire, and shelter, their greatest struggle is often mental—coping with the reality of being alone and isolated from society. Although participants endure the physical pain of hunger, it is often the emotional pain of missing family and loved ones compels some to tap out.

All of life can be summed up in one word: "Relationship." We have a relationship with God, a relationship with our spouse, a relationship with our family, a relationship with our friends, a relationship with our co-workers, and so on. Our physical and emotional health is nurtured through meaningful relationships.

When a marriage ends up in divorce due to infidelity, one or both spouses may experience the devouring beast of loneliness. Dr. Kevin Skinner, in his book *Treating Trauma from Sexual Betrayal,* quotes Dr. John Gottman, who observed, "Lonely people tend to let themselves be treated unfairly in order to be liked, but they also react with extreme suspicion about potential unfairness."[57]

Following a devastating experience of betrayal, lonely individuals often embark on a journey of withdrawal to avoid the pain of being hurt or betrayed again. Rather than choosing to love or trust again, they may opt for the pathway of isolation or loneliness.

Loneliness is quite different from being lonesome. A spouse may feel lonesome when their partner is away for an extended period. They mark the calendar, anxiously awaiting their spouse's return and the joy of being reunited. But loneliness isn't marked by a pencil; it's marked by a permanent marker. The marriage is over, the divorce papers are signed, and the separation is finalized. He is not coming back; she is not coming back, and you are alone.

How does one deal with persistent loneliness? Some people, like a turtle, withdraw into their shell. Their shell becomes their home, where they isolate themselves from others, brooding over the infidelity and wrestling with the strangling silence. Others are like the beaver, staying busy and constantly working. They fill their time with endless tasks and work long hours, avoiding home to escape the echoing emptiness. Their calendars are filled from Monday through Sunday. Even at home, they spend hours upon hours watching television and surfing the internet to distract themselves.

Yet another group of people resemble the boldness of an independent lion. They have reflected on their loss, embraced it, and moved beyond introspection. These individuals spring forward, daring to discover their new strength and boldly pursuing a new course for their lives.

The only cure for loneliness is to seek to establish new relationships, and the alone spouse must take that initiative. Dr. Gary Smalley, in his book *The DNA of Relationship*, referenced research by Dr. Dean Ornish on loneliness and isolation. His findings revealed that isolation and loneliness "increase the likelihood of disease and premature death from all causes by 200 to 500 percent or more.[58] Avoiding a lifestyle of isolation and deliberately seeking connection with others can significantly promote both emotional and physical healing.

Loneliness does not have to be a life sentence. If you are seeking to have an intimate relationship again, the desire is healthy, but it requires pursuing an intimate relationship should not be driven by a desire to escape loneliness.

It is essential to take time to build a solid spiritual foundation with God and become firmly grounded in His Word. A person also needs time to heal emotionally, psychologically, spiritually, socially, and, in some cases, physically. Additionally, it's important to achieve financial security and peace. A new relationship is like poured concrete—it takes time to set and become solid.

I want to encourage you, especially when you are struggling with loneliness, by reminding you that you are not alone. The writer of Hebrews, speaking about being content with what we have and avoiding covetousness, supplied the reason we can be content: "The Lord himself has said, I will never leave you nor forsake you." The Lord is better than anything we could possess—better than silver, gold, diamonds, or any form of wealth. Even if we do not have great financial wealth, we have the Lord Jesus Christ as our Savior, who is far more precious than any temporary wealth.

God also promised we are not alone when facing challenges. He said, "When you pass through the waters, I will be with thee; and through the rivers, they shall not overflow thee: When you walk through the fire you shall not be burned; neither shall the flame kindle upon thee" (Isaiah 43:2, NKJV). He is an infinitely great companion in life. Additionally, we have the promise of the Lord's continual presence, "And lo, I am with you always, even unto the end of the world" (Matthew 28:20, NKJV).

BETRAYED

The betrayed spouse struggles deeply with the betrayal, finding it difficult to believe when they have committed their life to their partner. The betrayal of trust brings an intensely painful emotional experience, accompanied by physical ramifications and psychological questions. These include the uncertainty of sociological and financial concerns, such as where and how one will live.

For example, both husband and wife must face the possibility of contracting a sexually transmitted disease, the emotional and financial trauma of a potential divorce, and, in some cases, the possibility of the woman with whom one's husband had a sexual relationship becoming pregnant.

Betrayal in marriage is like the crumbling of a piece of paper—it can never again be the same. Couples can move forward in forgiveness and grace, but the incident silently remains tucked away in their memory. While God may not take away the memory of the betrayal, He can enable us to address it as something that has been forgiven.

SHOCKED

When sexual betrayal is discovered, betrayed partners often go into deep shock, questioning, "How did I miss the signs?" or exclaiming, "I can't believe this is happening to me." They begin to question the reality or veracity of the discovery. The truth, once exposed, feels unfathomable and, for a moment, seems to be absurd.

The element of shock may stem from the careful, deliberate, and cautious planning of the unfaithful spouse to hide their infidelity. They were extremely skilled at living a double life and hiding their betrayal. Yet, what was hidden in the darkness for a time has been manifested in the light.

In King David's case, the revelation of his adultery with Bathsheba and the murder of Uriah was divinely orchestrated. Did David believe he had successfully covered his tracks? Was he shocked when the prophet Nathan exposed his notorious behavior?

HATE

Like anger, hate is a powerful emotion. The expression of hate often follows angry questions such as, "How could you? Didn't our marriage mean anything to you? What were you thinking? How could you hurt me like this?" After this tirade of questions, angry, negative comments may follow: "You piece of scum, you worthless piece of trash, you miserable loser!" Finally, the devasting betrayal is violently and succinctly stated, "I hate you," often followed by an explicit command, "Take your belongings and get out of this house!"

Many times, this strong expression of hate arises from the sudden and unsuspected betrayal, which blankets a love that, unexplainably, still exists towards the offending spouse.

Lewis B. Smedes, in his book *Forgive & Forget,* highlighted the difference between hate and anger. He wrote, "Anger is a sign that we are alive and well. Hate is a sign that we are sick a need to be healed." So, he felt that it is not anger that requires healing in our lives but rather hate that demands healing.[59]

Shirley P. Glass, in her book *Not "Just Friends,"* revealed that "Of the partners of sex addicts, 60 percent threatened to leave after the initial disclosure, but only 24 percent who threatened to leave actually left."[60] This is an indication that strongly expressed feelings during the initial discovery of infidelity may gradually subside as individuals process the situation, evaluate the strength of their commitment to each other, and consider the possibility of moving forward in reconciliation.

Perhaps the greatest triumph over the explosive emotion of hate is found in Paul's admonition to married couples: "Be kind to one another, tenderhearted, forgiving one another; even as God in Christ forgave you"

(Ephesians 4:32, NKJV). Granted, this is not something that automatically takes place but is a process. It involves understanding the undeserved forgiveness of Christ and His willingness to love the unlovely, processing the the pain of betrayal, and determining to work hard to salvage the marriage. Through God's enabling power, one can follow this admonition.

When you follow Paul's admonition and forgive the betraying spouse, releasing the hate stored within you, something very radical, powerful, and positive takes place in your life. "When you release the wrongdoer from the wrong, you cut a malignant tumor out of your inner life."[61]

Granted, while the one who betrayed you may experience a measure of freedom from guilt and shame through forgiveness, the greatest freedom is yours. You, once a chained prisoner of hate, are emotionally healed and set free!

REVENGE

In defining revenge, we shall look at Miriam Webster's definitions of the term, as both a verb and a noun. The verb form is defined as "to avenge (oneself or another) usually by retaliating in kind or degree, to inflict injury in return for *revenge* an insult."[62] The noun form is described as "a desire for vengeance or retribution motivated by *revenge*, an act or instance of retaliating in order to get even, an opportunity for getting satisfaction sought *revenge* through a rematch."[63]

A person of revenge characteristically possesses a desire to do harm or to punish someone for a perceived wrong done to them. Individuals often use the phrase "sweet revenge." However, Dale M. Kushner challenged this notion, stating, "Contrary to popular belief, revenge is rarely sweet! Nor does it automatically lead to catharsis or closure but instead invites continued brooding and dissatisfaction. Increased rumination sets the stage for retribution and more cycles of aggression."[64]

God gives clear counsel for a spouse whose heart may be filled with vengeance. Paul exhorted the Romans, "Recompense to no man evil for evil. Provide things honest in the sight of all men. If it be possible, as much as lieth in you, live peaceably with all men. Dearly beloved, avenge not yourselves, but rather give place unto wrath; for it is written, 'Vengeance is mine: I will repay, saith the Lord'" (Romans 12:17-19, KJV).

King Solomon declared, "Whoever digs a pit will fall into it; if someone rolls a stone, it will roll back on them" (Proverbs 26:2, NLT). An often quoted saying by Confucius, a 5th-century Chinese philosopher, reminds us: "Before you embark on a journey of revenge, dig two graves." In other words, harboring an attitude of bitterness and revenge not only seeks to hurt another but ultimately causes harm to us.

OVERWHELMED

For some, the discovery of infidelity feels overwhelming, like standing in a foot of water along the beach when a giant wave suddenly appears and knocks you down, leaving you gasping for air. This is a serious and consuming emotion. Negative thoughts, like the ocean wave, flood your mind, causing you to question your self-worth, your purpose, and your future.

But these overwhelming feelings must not be allowed to cloud your reasoning and inhibit sound judgment. Your life has a purpose! You were created by God on purpose for a purpose.

You cannot control the actions and behavior of another person, but you can—and must— control your reaction and behavior to the discovery of infidelity. This may necessitate reaching out to a good friend, a pastor, a licensed counselor, or a psychologist for substantial emotional support.

Amid your despair, you may find great consolation by calling out to God. David said, "In my distress I cried unto the Lord, and he heard me and delivered me from all my fears" (Psalm 120: 1, KJV).

STRESSED

Dr. Tim Clinton and Dr. Mark Laaser in their book *Sexuality & Relationship Counseling,* wrote, "...More than 80 percent of physician office visits are associated with unresolved stress issues."[65] Many couples navigating the aftermath of sexual infidelity experience heightened stress levels greater than at almost any other time in their lives.

Stress is our emotional response to circumstances that are challenging or demanding. When under stress, you may feel as though your life is falling apart. Psychologists agree that when stress occurs, that our physical bodies respond in one of three ways: fight, flight, or freeze.

When stress is experienced over long periods, the body produces high levels of cortisol, which can become toxic and impair the immune system. The irony is that our human bodies can navigate stress for some time without us paying much attention to its effects, because stress, for the most part, comes and goes. However, prolonged stress eventually leads to both minor and major impairments.

Dan B. Allender observed, "Our body is beautifully designed to immediately and effectively gear up for short bouts of stress, but we are not designed to continue operating at that crazy accelerated pace." [66]

Dr. Pierce J. Howard stated, "Minor results of this stress-related impairment include colds, flu, backaches, tight chest, migraine headaches, tension headaches, allergy outbreaks, and skin ailments."[67] He further noted that life-threatening conditions may include "hypertension, ulcers, accidental proneness, addictions, asthma, infertility, colon or bowel disorders, diabetes, kidney disease, rheumatoid arthritis, and mental illness."[68]

In addition, Howard wrote, "Chronic stress can result in energy depletion, depression, insecurity, impotence or frigidity, apathy, emotional withdrawal, insomnia, chronic fatigue, helplessness or hopelessness, anxiety, confusion, lack of concentration, and poor memory."[69]

I would like to offer you three verses to meditate on (or memorize) to help you to navigate stress.

Jeremiah wrote, "For I know the thoughts that I think toward you says the Lord, thoughts of peace and not of evil, to give you a future and a hope" (Jeremiah 29:11, NKJV).

Jesus said, "Therefore do not worry about tomorrow, for tomorrow will worry about its own things. Sufficient for the day is its own trouble" (Matthew 6:34, NKJV).

Paul the Apostle encouraged the Romans, "And we know that all things work together for good to those who love God, to those who are called according to his purposes" (Romans 8:28, NKJV).

MOURNING

People often associate mourning with the death of a loved one. However, mourning is an aspect of grief that can include recovering from various types of loss. For example, it may involve recovering from the death of a family pet, moving to a strange place and losing daily contact with friends, going through a devastating breakup with a boyfriend or girlfriend, experiencing the betrayal of your spouse, losing a job, or failing to reach a goal.

The process of mourning over a loss is contingent upon the severity of the loss and the individual's ability to navigate it. For instance, mourning the death of a loved one may last between six and twenty months. Mourning the loss of a spouse due to infidelity does not have to end in despair. Instead, it can become a healing process for one's emotional, psychological, and physical health.

As we conclude the first part of this book, let me state other emotions could have been included, but what is most important is that we seek to discover, identify, and not ignore our emotions. Peter Scazzero, quoting Dan Allender and Tremper Longman in their book, *The Cry of the Soul,* wrote, "Ignoring our emotions is turning our back or reality. Listening to our emotions ushers us into reality. And reality is where we meet God..."[70]

And as you commit to being honest with yourself and with God, you will discover incremental change taking place in your heart, mind, soul, and spirit.

PART 2

DEFINING INFIDELITY

Infidelity is intricately and deceitfully woven into the moral fabric of our society. Defining infidelity is not as simple as one may think. Are there different types of infidelity? Is infidelity solely as having sexual intercourse? Is one type of infidelity more severe than another? What about a one-night stand? Does emotional infidelity exist? Is viewing pornography while married an act of infidelity? What about sexting? Can cybersex be considered infidelity?

Esther Perel, wrote, "The definition of infidelity is anything but fixed, and the digital age offers an ever-expanding range of poetically illicit encounters."[71] Dr. Lindal Mintle defined infidelity as, "A breach of trust, a breaking of the covenant, a betrayal of a relationship."[72] If I were to paint with broad brushstrokes, I would concur with Dr. L.H. Baucom who stated, "Infidelity is a major upheaval in a committed relationship. It breaks the bond of trust and invades the safety of that relationship."[73]

By embracing Baucom's definition, it becomes clear that any of the above-mentioned scenarios would irrefutably fall under the category of infidelity.

I would like to present a long quote from Michelle Mays' book, *The Betrayal Bind,* in which one may readily see that betrayal is more than breaking a trust or a covenant relationship with your spouse—it may also be a trauma one must navigate.

> A simple definition of trauma comes from Dr. Norman Wright, who defined trauma as a separation from safety. This elegantly sums up what happens when we experience betrayal. We are instantly separated from our sense of safe connections with our significant other, who has suddenly become dangerous and painful.[74]

Maybe Job did not set out to define pornography, but when he said, "I made a covenant with my eyes not to look lustfully (having a strong sexual desire) at a young woman" (Job 31:1), he captured its essence. Similarly, Christ, while addressing adultery, (physical/sexual infidelity), expanded its scope beyond the physical act to include the mindset of committing adultery in one's heart

(Matthew 5:28, KJV). Jesus emphasized that our attitude and thoughts can be just as sinful as our physical acts.

PHYSICAL/SEXUAL FIDELITY

The first type of infidelity, generally acknowledged without debate, is the physical/sexual betrayal of one's partner. Throughout history, such betrayal has been defined as adultery. The seventh commandment explicitly prohibits the act of adultery (Exodus 20:14).

Adultery was viewed by Jesus Christ as a *justifiable* reason for the innocent partner in a marriage relationship to annul the marriage covenant. Jesus said, "But I say unto you, that whosoever shall put away his wife (i.e. divorce) saving for the cause of fornication, causeth her to commit adultery: and whosoever shall marry her that is divorced committeth adultery" (Matthew 5:32, KJV).

An adulterer is a man who engages in illicit sexual intercourse with a married woman, while an adulteress is a woman who engages in illicit sexual intercourse with a married man. In other words, adultery is a voluntary sexual act between a married person (husband or wife) and someone other than their spouse.

There are various descriptive words used to soften the devasting impact of adultery and its immoral behavior.

Some reference adultery as "cheating," on "having an affair," or dismissively calling it "just a one-night fling."

There are those who embrace moral relativism and others who adhere to absolute moralism. A very simplistic understanding of moral relativism is the often-heard expression, "When in Rome, do as Romans do." Behind this expression lies the belief that there are no universal moral absolutes. Individuals with this mindset often feel incompetent to judge others and make a clear distinction between moral and cultural standards or beliefs. From the perspective of a moral relativist, an adulterous betrayal might be dismissed as insignificant, something that "just happened."

In contrast, absolute moralism believes there are moral laws, and these laws are universal, unconditional, and unaffected by one's cultural beliefs and external circumstances.

Michele Weiner-Davis revealed in a recent study a comparison between French and American views of infidelity. Whereas 47 percent of the French population believed that an affair was immoral, 84% of Americans believed that having an affair was immoral.[75] This comparison illustrates aspects of moral relativism and absolute moralism in the 21st century.

Conservative theologians view adultery as a sin, referencing Exodus 20:14, and assert that such sin is subject to the wrath of God. David, after his sin with Bathsheba and the murder of her husband, Uriah, recognized that his actions were not only against them but ultimately against God. He confessed, "Against thee, and thee only have I sinned and done this evil in thy sight: that thou mightest be justified when thou speakest and be clear when thou judgest" (Psalm 51:4, KJV).

Betrayal is a much more accurate word, for it deals not only with the physical, but also the emotional, psychological, social, legal, and spiritual dynamics of the relationship. "Betrayal always creates relational disconnections."[76] The agony of betrayal changes the dynamic of who we are, shifting us from being whole, secure, competent, content, and loved to feeling wounded, afraid, uncertain, discontent, unloved, and humiliated.

Any sexual act outside of marriage exposes one to the imminent danger of contracting a sexually transmitted disease. Though it may be uncomfortable to see a medical doctor, wisdom dictates that you do so—for peace of mind and, if necessary, to receive appropriate medical attention.

Financially, there is also the possibility of one losing one's job, especially if both are employed in the same company. The financial impact may, in some cases lead to bankruptcy or require spending thousands of dollars for a divorce.

In one's social environment, there is the potential risk of physical retaliation by an angry spouse, which could escalate to criminal activity.

The emotional trauma following the discovery of infidelity cannot easily be dismissed, as it often leads to the pursuit of therapy and counseling. We cannot dismiss the possibility of pregnancy, which adds stress, anxiety, and financial responsibilities.

In addition, there is the psychological impact of dealing with guilt, shame, and diminished self-worth, as well as the spiritual impact of transgressing the moral law of God and offending a holy God.

EMOTIONAL INFIDELITY

You may or may not be familiar with the term "emotional affair." Emotional affairs, which involve limited sexual intimacy without intercourse, comprise about "20 percent of those who admit to infidelity."[77] Other studies reveal that "22 % of men and 14% of women commit emotional or physical infidelity."[78]

An individual engaged in an emotional connection with a person of the opposite sex who is not their spouse may assume that, because there was no sexual intercourse, they are not guilty of infidelity. Esther Perel described an emotional affair as an "inappropriate emotional closeness" that should be reserved for one's spouse and depletes the primary relationship.[79]

I may not know the depth of emotion a man experiences when he looks at a woman to lust after her, but I do believe that lust contributes to powerful feelings that overtake him, leading to a heightened sense of emotional excitement. Jesus declared that whoever looks on a woman to lust hath committed adultery with her in his heart (Matthew 5:28, KJV).

Dr. Shirley P. Glass, an infidelity expert, noted in her clinical sample that 85 percent of women and 58 percent of men who did have sexual intercourse in an affair stated that they had strong or deep emotional attachment.[80]

Perhaps one of the best definitive statements concerning the occurrence of emotional infidelity is given by Subbotnik and Harris, "Emotional infidelity occurs between two people who form secret passionate connections outside of the marriage."[81] Rokach and Chan quoted Leeker and Carlozzi who viewed emotional infidelity as "The occurrence of emotional involvement with a third party that violates the ground rules established by the couple…".[82]

Such emotional connections may develop when texting, talking, emailing, or having that seemingly "innocent" cup of coffee with a person of the opposite sex. They may also occur while working long hours on the job site with an attractive colleague, exchanging a flirtatious wink, sharing a ride with the opposite sex to a work assignment, or offering excessive flattery. Other examples include reconnecting with an ex-husband or ex-wife, engaging with an old boyfriend or girlfriend on social media, giving a prolonged hug, using sexually suggestive language, having long conversations, or sharing one's thoughts and feelings.

An emotional affair may also manifest in becoming more committed to another individual than to your spouse, "slow dancing to the music" with someone who is not your spouse, sharing breaks at work, scheduling after-work engagements, or spending money on the individual.

A person is headed down a slippery slope when they persistently hide these emotional connections. Such actions may also be compared to walking through a minefield—one step from death or serious injury. Refusing to recognize the potential dangers of this emotional minefield often leads to the destruction of a marriage. Even if the marriage survives, emotional infidelity leaves scars that take many years to heal.

Shirley P. Glass, commenting on emotional affairs as being "characterized by secrecy, emotional intimacy, and sexual chemistry" expressed that they "can be more threatening than brief sexual flings".[83]

Before leaving the subject of emotional infidelity, it is important to note that this infidelity has five noticeable stages. The duration of these stages may vary from couple to couple.

The Communication Stage

The first stage is the communication stage, which may begin innocently—perhaps a casual conversation over a cup of coffee or meeting a friend of your spouse at a social engagement. However, the communication continues, and you begin to share personal and intimate information about yourself—details that should remain between you and your spouse. Sharing such intimate communications fuels the fire of a perceived special bond, and increasingly more time is dedicated to these interactions.

The Concealing Stage

Infidelity often progresses from casual connections and continuous correspondence to secretive calendar commitments. Meetings are coordinated around work schedules, a post office box may be obtained for credit card billing associated with a newly acquired credit card, and passcodes are installed on phones. Lying becomes a necessity, quickly evolving into a lifestyle of deception.

The foundation of a marriage, built on trust, truth, and transparency, is eroded daily by the flood waters of deception. Many victims of sexual infidelity have oft commented that the lying was even more devastating than the act of infidelity itself.

The Connecting Stage

At this stage, the concealment phase begins to expose itself. Increasing amounts of time are spent openly connecting in public. Perhaps it's having lunch together in restaurants, attending sports events, coincidentally showing up at the same movie theater, and standing in line together to purchase tickets. All kinds of scenarios are fostered during this stage.

As more boundaries are crossed, they are often rationalized, dismissed, denied, or challenged as absurd if detected.

The Commitment Stage

In this stage, fantasy becomes an all-consuming passion, and physical sexual desire escalates to the point where all moral restraints are abandoned. Selfish pleasure overrides reason, integrity, loyalty, and common sense, with little thought given to the consequences of the sensual and adulterous act of betrayal.

The Confrontational Stage

It may take time for the innocent spouse to painstakingly gather all the facts, but more often than not, sexual infidelity is eventually discovered. When this happens, there is often more fancy twisting of the truth than iron in the hands of a blacksmith. The exposed spouse typically responds with a deluge of denials.

Only when the evidence is undeniably corroborated does the offending spouse admit the truth. In some cases, the guilty party endeavors to shift the blame onto their spouse rather than accepting full responsibility for their actions.

ONE NIGHT SEXUAL FLING

In contrast to emotional infidelity, sexual infidelity is often referred to as a "one-night fling" and quickly minimized by the guilty husband. He may dismiss it as a sexual act that "did not mean anything," quickly rationalize it claiming he had "one too many drinks," or shift blame by saying that "the woman seduced him." Additionally, he may declare his love for his wife and emphasize that he was not "emotionally involved" with the other woman.

Schneider, commenting on the language men often use to describe promiscuous sexual success with women, revealed the objectification of women. He concluded that it is not surprising many men grow up embracing a mindset that views casual affairs as a "minor matter," with a one-night stand carrying no more significance "than eating an extra dessert."[84]

Some sexual flings remain hidden for years and, in some cases, may never be revealed, often due to the lack of an ongoing emotional attachment. However, one-night flings are exposed when, for instance, the woman becomes pregnant and refuses to have an abortion. At that point, the secrecy ends, and there is no more hiding.

One-night flings may also be discovered when the offending party is diagnosed by a medical doctor with a sexually transmitted disease.

No matter how one tries to downplay the sexual infidelity of a one-night fling, the innocent party will experience an emotional wound. While the pain of any infidelity should not be minimized, a one-night fling and a long-term betrayal may be compared to a first-degree burn, which is painfully sore, and a fourth-degree burn, which is life-threatening. The intensity of the emotional pain differs significantly.

For example, the pain of discovering a spouse's one-night encounter with a stranger at an airport may be less intense than the emotional devastation caused by uncovering a seven-year affair with one's closest friend or neighbor. However, in some cases, the emotional wound of a one-night fling may feel more severe, especially when layers of lies must be tenaciously uncovered to reveal the truth.

Solomon viewed the extreme folly of sexual immorality when he wrote, "Suddenly he follows her as an ox goes to the slaughter, or as one in fetters to the discipline of a fool, Until an arrow pierces through his liver, As a bird hastens to the snare, So he does not know that it will cost him his life" (Proverbs 7:22-23, NASB).

FRIENDS WITH BENEFITS

Friends with benefits (FWBs) occurs when two people, who are friends, rationalize occasional sexual experiences by insisting they are not in love with each other, though they may have special feelings for one another. They feel entirely free to date other individuals.

In some scenarios, individuals claim they feel safer having sex with a friend but do not want the responsibilities of a committed relationship. FWBs is like a helium balloon with no strings attached, freely drifting away from your fingers. It stands in stark contrast to the committed covenant relationship between a man and a woman.

There are many dangers in such a relationship. As with any sexual relationship outside of marriage, there is the risk of contracting sexually transmitted diseases, especially if one friend is also engaging in sexual relationships with others. There is the danger of an unplanned pregnancy.

Another danger lies in unexpressed personal expectations. One person may hope for the relationship to continue and evolve into a deeper commitment, while the other does not share the same feelings, fostering false hope. Additionally, the individual seeking a deeper connection may become angry or resentful if the arrangement to ends, particularly if they have fallen in love.

Jealousy is another potential danger, especially if either individual begins dating someone else while maintaining the arrangement too.

In essence, FWBs is fornication when practiced by unmarried individuals, or adultery if a married individual becomes unfaithful to their spouse. Such infidelity is destined to be very destructive in any marriage. The emphasis of the relationship is self-serving, prioritizing the fulfillment of physical and sexual needs without any emotional commitment to the other person. "Only about 10-20% of FWBs turn into long romantic relationships."[85]

CYBER INFIDELITY

To some, the term *cyber infidelity* may be unfamiliar, but to those familiar with using a computer, it is not only familiar but may describe a form of infidelity occurring within their marriage. Cyber infidelity (sometimes referred to as Cyber Sex) occurs when a spouse withdraws emotionally and physically from sexual intimacy with their partner and intentionally substitutes it with interactions on a computer. This involves two people engaging in sexually suggestive conversations, texts, or images, with the intended goal of bringing each other to sexual climax, thereby violating a sacred commitment made to their spouse.

Simply speaking, cyber infidelity is yet another form of betrayal of the trust once committed to one's spouse. It is an intentional and insidious invitation extended to others in cyberspace.

Cyber infidelity, like emotional infidelity, shares the common denominator of the absence of any physical/sexual relationship. Proponents and participants of Cyber Sex argue that they are not guilty of sexual infidelity because no physical contact is involved. But as with any betrayal of trust within a marriage, they are still guilty of infidelity.

Participants place themselves in a vulnerable situation, as ongoing correspondence with individuals in cyberspace may lead to a scheduled rendezvous with the Cyber Sex partner.

PORNOGRAPHY—THE NEW INFIDELITY

I encourage readers to be cognizant of the 100-billion-dollar pornography industry and to consider the following statistics reported in 2020.

Porn hub boasted of:

- 42 billion visits in a year.
- 113 million daily visits.
- 170 years' worth of new content created.[86]
- 2.5 billion emails are sent that contain pornographic material.
- 68 million searches are related to pornography.
- 116,000 searches are specifically for child pornography.[87]

As we look at this new infidelity, we must begin by defining pornography. Those who view pornography often seek to justify their inordinate affections and lustful desires by challenging theologians, judges, ministers, sex therapists, husbands, or wives regarding the definition of pornography.

Bev Hislop, in her book *Shepherding Women in Pain*, defined pornography as, "sexually explicit material: films, magazines writings, photographs, or other materials that are sexually explicit and intended to cause sexual arousal."[88]

In 1970, the U.S. Presidential Commission on Obscenity and Pornography presented a general interpretation of pornography, describing it as "any sexually explicit material capable of arousing sexual arousal."[89] However, in 1972, the Longford Report offered a more precise definition: "That which exploits and dehumanizes sex so that human beings are treated as things and women in particular as sex objects."[90]

Christianity opposes the debasement of sexuality that pornography promotes. It upholds that sex was given by God as a means for human beings, male and female, to mutually express their love for one another within a committed relationship, finding fulfillment and connection through that physical and sexual bond.

The viewing of pornography in our today's culture by children, teens, and adults has become not only a recreational "go-to" but also a default mechanism for coping with anger, frustration, anxiety, rejection, and self-worth issues. In some cases, it even facilitates a sense of control for the narcissistic person.

The anonymity, affordability, and availability of pornography on the internet have turned it into a multi-billion-dollar industry. This accessibility has significantly eroded moral boundaries and contributed to a hedonistic mindset in society, where pornography is increasingly rationalized as the norm.

Judith A. Reisman, commenting on the impact of internet pornography, declared, "A 'civil war' is being waged sabotaging the most vulnerable Americans at home, at work, on our streets, in our libraries, and on our campuses everywhere."[91]

Sam Black, in his book *The Healing Church*, referencing the 2014 Barna Research survey, revealed that "88 percent of men" had been exposed to pornography by the "age of fifteen."[92] Today, over ten years later. we can reasonably predict an even higher rate of exposure, with many marriages suffering because of one spouse consuming pornography and sexually acting out in selfish pleasure.

Mark Laaser, writing over twenty years ago in his book *Healing the Wounds of Sexual Addiction,* stated that various studies revealed that "two-thirds of Christian men" have visited pornography sites on the Internet.[93] In 2003, Clifford and Joyce Penner wrote that 137 million websites referenced the subject of sex, and most of them were centered around pornographic content. They noted that such sites are increasing at a rate of 1,000,000 a month.[94]

With the plethora of pornographic sites available today, and men and women engaging in masturbation while viewing such content, pornography has become what many refer to as *the new infidelity* or the *silent infidelity*[95] It sabotages marriages by eroding times of intimacy, pleasure, and the sexual bond that God intended within marriage, while simultaneously creating pathways to sexual addiction, and, ultimately, *sexual infidelity*.

Dr. Robert Weiss defines infidelity (cheating) as "the breaking of trust that occurs when you keep intimate, meaningful secrets from your primary romantic partner." Ted Shimer further described pornography as "a gateway drug to adultery."[97] He also referenced two studies from *Psychology Today* that revealed pornography is responsible for about 500,000 divorces in the United States. Additionally, the studies found that if one partner views pornography, the couple is two to three times more likely to divorce within two years compared to couples who do not view porn.[98]

Bev Hislop wrote, "Pornography ensnares participants, corrupts lives, and destroys relationships. It results in various unnatural manifestations of sexual desire, including, but not limited to prostitution, pornographic magazines/ videos/pictures/ Internet sites, masturbation, topless bars, strip clubs, adultery/fornication, and rape."[99]

Individuals caught up in such a lifestyle, who become sexual addicts, spend less and less time with their spouse, dedicating more and more time to pursuing their sexual fantasies.

Women whose husbands are addicted to pornography often lament they cannot compete with a multitude of women portrayed on multiple porn sites—women with seemingly flawless skin, voluptuous figures, and perfect hairstyles, who are viewed by their husbands hour after hour, day by day. As a result, these women increasingly feel sexually abandoned, emotionally rejected, and physically isolated.

In their book *Safe Haven Marriage*, Dr. Archibald Hart and Sharon May commented on how a woman views pornography. "For a woman, pornography is a slap in the face and a stab in the heart. It says to her that she is not good enough, not worthy enough, and not attractive to be the source of her spouse's sexual attention."[100]

Dr. James Dobson, a prominent Christian licensed psychologist who served on the Attorney General's Commission on Pornography during the 1980s, wrote, "If people understood the debauchery of this business, and what pornography does to the individual addicted to it, they would be more motivated to work for its control."[101]

It is heartbreaking to see marriages shattered by sexual infidelity, where, in many cases, pornography was a contributing factor. Paradise Creek Recovery Center made the following statement, "We understand the beast of sex addiction. Likewise, we know the path of porn addiction can lead to infidelity."[102]

Ted Shimer sounds the alarm to every church and Christian denomination in America, boldly declaring, "This porn problem is destroying Christian marriages, enslaving the next generation of Christian leaders, and helping to produce pedophile pastors."[103]

To substantiate the fact that pornography is having a devastating impact on the church, he referenced a 2019

Houston Chronicle article with the headline, "More than 100 Southern Baptist Youth Pastors Convicted or Charged in Sex Crimes." The tragedy is that many, if not most, of these sex crimes reportedly "involved minors."[104]

SEXTING

Sexting is a term that originated in the digital era, referring to the use of cell phones to send, forward, and receive sexually explicit pictures, videos, or text messages between individuals or groups. In a monogamous marriage, where couples commit to each other for life, sexting would be considered a betrayal of that sacred trust.

Sharing sexual images with strangers outside of marriage not only stimulates sexual fantasy and excitement with someone outside the marriage covenant but also constitutes emotional infidelity. Moreover, sexting may lead to sexual infidelity, further violating the marital bond.

Psychology Today highlighted research on sexting, revealing that only about 12 percent of adults in established relationships engage in sexting. The low percentage among this group is attributed to concerns about the risk of a third party viewing their sexts.[105]

In contrast, statistics reveal that 50 to 60 percent of younger adults engage in sexting.[106] Nicole Artz, a Licensed Family Marriage Therapist (LFMT), noted that 75 percent of individuals who engage in sexting consider it a form of cheating.[107]

The extreme and horrid danger of sexting lies in its illegality for individuals under the age of 18. Teenagers in dating relationships can face betrayal and bullying when such images are shared online. Once uploaded, these images can spread rapidly on the internet, leading to devastating consequences.

Marlynn Wei, writing for *Psychology Today*, revealed that "new **research,** published in the *Journal of Cyberpsychology, Behavior, and Social Networking* suggests that unwanted and nonconsensual sexting, which often includes images, has been linked with **depression, anxiety, and stress.**"[108]

PART 3
DEALING WITH HEALING

"Healing doesn't mean the damage never existed. It means the damage no longer controls our life."[109]

- AUTHOR UNKNOWN

Perhaps one of the most challenging questions you may be asking is, "How do I find healing from the painful stabbing wound of infidelity in which trust has been broken?"

As a boy, I lived in the hills of rural West Virginia. The roads were winding, filled with sharp curves that ascended and descended mountains, marked by numerous caution signs and speed limit signs. Navigating the mountainous topography was a challenge and necessitated time. The roads were not straight, allowing for quick or effortlessly travel, but zig-zagged around the terrain.

I use this as an illustration to emphasize that the healing process also takes time. Like those mountain roads, you will encounter many emotional curves and face numerous challenges. However, you can navigate this journey together, rebuild trust, and find joy in life again. Do not give up hope.

The practical questions couples often ask are, "If my marriage is salvageable and reconciliation is the goal, how long will it take? When will we find healing?" No counselor, psychologist, or marriage therapist can provide the correct answer.

This is because, just as no two snowflakes are alike, no two fingerprints are identical, and no two leaves on a tree are the same, there are no two marriages that are exactly alike. You are unique, your spouse is unique, your strengths are unique, and your relationship is unique.

However, the process of reconciliation can progress more quickly in some cases, depending on the sincere investment and commitment each spouse is willing to make.

Dr. Kathy Nickerson, in her book *The Courage to Stay,* stated that in her practice, most couples reported feeling "mostly better" after about nine months. She also highlighted that clinical research reveals that many couples take one to two years to heal from the affair.[110]

Michelle Weimer-Davis wrote, "Some people will find their relationship has normalized, and even improved within a few months.[111] For others, it may take years. Every couple is different, and timelines vary depending on the specific circumstances and issues they face."

Michelle Mays, a licensed Professional counselor wrote in her book *The Betrayal Blind* that once betrayed partners gain a fuller understanding of the issues surrounding the betrayal, they begin to recognize there is no quick fix. Healing from betrayal, she explained, is a "longer-term process of learning about the repairing of the wounds that have occurred."[112]

Every individual deal with the healing process in different ways. However, certain elements of commonality are often present in the pursuit of healing. As we move forward in this journey, it is paramount that we remain honest with ourselves about our thought processes as they relate to healing.

We examine five key areas of healing: Emotional healing, spiritual healing, psychological healing, physical healing, and social healing. These may sometimes overlap. For example, the process of forgiving can involve both emotional and spiritually dimensions.

STEPS OF EMOTIONAL HEALING

In the first chapter, we spent considerable time identifying and briefly discussing a variety of negative emotions that surface when infidelity is discovered, along with some thoughts on addressing specific emotions. In this section, I have provided ways people can find emotional healing.

Before reviewing these approaches, it is important to realize that people process emotions differently. For example, intellectually and volitionally, a person can declare, "I forgive you," but the emotional component of forgiveness often takes time. The deeper the hurt, the slower the process of emotional healing.

Timelines for emotional healing vary greatly, and an offending spouse should not falsely assume that their partner can quickly forgive and move on. Healing is not instantaneous. For example, the difference between a scratch, which can heal in a matter of days, and a broken arm, which requires weeks, illustrates how some wounds take much longer to mend.

Some individuals may need time alone and to process their emotions. The idea of sitting down to connect and communicate may feel overpowering. In such cases, it is wise to express your intention to connect and communicate soon but emphasize that, at this moment, you simply need time and space to identify and process your emotions.

Informing your partner of your intentions is essential because, as the offended spouse, you need to have conversations about the affair. These discussions provide an opportunity for your painful feelings to be validated and your tormenting questions to be answered. They also allow the offending spouse to express their thoughts, feelings, and plans.

Ultimately, refusing to connect and communicate at the appropriate time will almost certainly hinder the restoration of your marriage.

Let me encourage you in the process of emotional healing. There will be sunny days where you feel bright and cheerful and cloudy days where you feel down. In other words, you will experience emotional highs and lows. It is crucial not to lose hope and to recognize that these shifting emotions are part of your healing journey and can be beneficial.

EXPRESS YOUR FEELINGS BY CRYING

We cry when we are physically hurt, and we cry when we are emotionally hurt. Physical pain is often treated with prescription painkillers, binding wounds, or setting broken bones. However, emotional wounds can produce tears that seem to fill buckets, with no quick fixes. Yet, the tears we shed are therapeutic. Crying is a healthy way to express the hurt, agony, and suffocating sadness you feel.

You need to allow yourself the freedom to cry whenever you feel like crying. In other words, permit yourself to let those tears flow—they are an essential part of your healing.

After the announcement and discovery of infidelity, you may have found yourself crying for weeks or even months. Perhaps you cried upon waking up or before going to bed. You might have cried before going to work, while driving, or even during the workday. The tears may have seemed endless.

Throughout the year, special events like Mother's Day, Father's Day, birthdays, and graduations might have triggered sudden bursts of tears. Holidays such as Thanksgiving and Christmas may have brought on tears that flowed effortlessly. You may have found yourself crying in public places—the local market, at the mall, your children's activities and sports events, restaurants, church, or even in the homes of family members and friends.

It is almost impossible to avoid circumstances, scenes, smells, pictures, expressions, occasions, events, words, or things that trigger our memories during the healing process from betrayal. Life is a collection of memories, with each one either positively or negatively imprinted and stored in our brains. Sexual betrayal forms a profoundly negative memory, often juxtaposed with years of loving memories and mutual trust.

Brian Becker, an associate professor of neuropsychology at Lesley University, defines memory as "the process in which the mind interprets, stores, and retrieves information."[113] During the grieving process, certain bits of information we have interpreted and stored are retrieved, often evoking emotional responses and bringing tears to the surface.

Cindy Beall, in her book *Healing Your Marriage When Trust Is Broken,* shared that when the tears came, she did not restrain them. She stated, "If I learned anything about allowing this, it is that if you don't stop the tears when they need to fall, they eventually stop themselves."[114] Her insights offer clarity: tears will flow, but if you allow them, the flood of tears will eventually subside.

During the healing process, some triggers may still cause a few tears to fall, but over time, they will no longer result in uncontrollable rivers of tears.

SHOW REMORSE

Remorse is a powerful and precious salve that an offending spouse can apply to the emotional wound of their betrayed partner. While processing the hurt of infidelity, it is important to acknowledge that the source of the hurt is someone the innocent spouse has deeply loved. The presence of the offending spouse may feel like the proverbial "elephant in the room," bringing discomfort and pain. Yet, their presence is also essential for the healing process.

Despite the discomfort their presence may bring, the offending spouse has a golden opportunity to facilitate and expedite healing by demonstrating genuine remorse. This involves adopting a sincere demeanor and offering heartfelt words of apology that truly reflect the depth of their regret and understanding of the pain they have caused.

In most cases, the innocent spouse may find some comfort in listening to the sincere remorse expressed by their partner. This heartfelt apology can serve as an emotional salve, contributing to their healing as they recognize their spouse's genuine sorrow for the pain inflicted by their betrayal.

From a practical perspective, it is difficult for a spouse to consider forgiving the sexual betrayal if there is no sincere demonstration of remorse. A natural thought might arise: "How can I trust that my spouse will not act out again if they show no remorse now?" While remorse never earns forgiveness—since forgiveness is a volitional act—it often provides reassurance and facilitates the healing process.

Depending on the personality and emotional maturity of the offending spouse, their sincere apology may be accompanied by authentic tears. Ironically, such expressions of remorse may also offer the offending spouse an opportunity to unburden themselves of the amassed amount of guilt and shame they carry.

Dr. Gary Chapman, in his book *When Sorry Isn't Enough*, stated, "Apology is birthed in the womb of regret."[115] Such sincere regret speaks volumes to the offended spouse because it demonstrates that the offending spouse is accepting responsibility for their actions. This is especially meaningful when the offending spouse specifically defines the action or actions they regret, making the apology both clear and personal.

PRACTICE EMPATHY

After the shock of discovering infidelity, when the vitriolic voices have been silenced, anger has cooled, retaliations have been abandoned, painful periods of questioning and answering have ceased, explanations have been given, truth has been revealed, love has been evaluated, sincere apologies have been made, remorse has been demonstrated, and the affair has ended, both the offending spouse and the innocent spouse may find themselves in need of a rich supply of empathy.

What is empathy? Alexandra Katehakis, a licensed marriage and family therapist, defined empathy as, "Your ability to recognize feel, and experience another person's thoughts and moods."[116] Psychiatrist Alfred Adler defined empathy as, "Seeing with the eyes of another, listening with the ears of another, and feeling with the heart of another."[117] Joel P. Bretscher and Kenneth C. Hauck, in their book *The Gift of Empathy,* pointed out its essential qualities. "Empathy is looking at the world from someone else's perspective to experience what the person is feeling—and then expressing your understanding of those feelings to that person."[118]

Brene Brown further explained the depth of empathy, writing, "No one reaches out to you for compassion or empathy so you can teach them how to behave better. They reach out to us because they believe in our capacity to know our darkness well enough to sit in the dark with."[119]

There is an urgent need for someone to provide understanding and demonstrate empathy to the hurting spouse during the sudden and painful discovery of infidelity. The wounded person faces seemingly insurmountable problems and is left wondering, "who can I share my story with?" Steven Covey aptly stated, "When you show deep empathy towards others their defensive energy goes down, and positive energy replaces it. That's when you can get more creative in solving problems."[120]

It is important to distinguish between empathy and sympathy. Sympathy connotes a compelling compassionate feeling toward a person, often perceived as pity. In contrast, empathy involves not only sharing in another person's feelings but also engaging in "an imaginative reconstruction of the situation's meaning for the other person based on the empathizer's experience of similar situations."[121] In short, emphasizers *feel with* someone, while sympathizers *feel for* them.[122] Sympathy expresses concern or care toward a person but refuses to build a bridge of personal involvement into their world, whereas empathy steps fully into the other's experience.

Stephen Covey defined sympathy as a "form of agreement, a form of judgment." He distinguished it from empathetic listening, which he described as not necessarily agreeing with someone but instead fully and deeply understanding a person both emotionally and intellectually.[123] Covey emphasized the therapeutic and healing value of empathy, explaining that when you listen with empathy, you provide the other person with "psychological air." He understood that while a human being's greatest need is physical survival, the next most vital need is psychological survival, which he defined as being understood, affirmed, and appreciated.[124]

INCORPORATE POSITIVE EMOTIONS

Dr. Fredrickson, in her article titled *"What Good Are Positive Emotions,"* pointed out that positive emotions broaden the scope of cognition and action, and build physical, intellectual, and social resources.[125]

Dr. Jennifer Steller presented a fascinating TED MED talk in 2015 entitled *"The Positive Effects of Positive Emotions."* She emphasized that positive emotions such as compassion, joy, love, and awe have profound effects on the physical health of an individual. Her research looked at some important markers of immune-functioning proteins called "pro-inflammatory cytokines," which serve as regulators of one's immune system. These were noted to promote inflammation in response to infection, illness, or injury. While small in size, these proteins are linked to acute symptoms like fever, fatigue, and pain. Dr. Stellar also stated that, over time, these proteins contribute to chronic conditions such as diabetes, cardiovascular disease, and depression.[126]

Her research focused on one of the many different types of pro-inflammatory cytokines, called "Interleukin's" or "IL 6," showing that positive emotions were associated with lower levels of pro-inflammatory cytokines. In addition, she pointed out four specific emotions—joy, pride, contentment, and awe—with awe rating as the strongest of the four.[127]

I find this very interesting. David, who lived from 1040 BCE to 970 BCE, must have experienced the positive emotional effect of awe when he declared, "When I considered your heavens, the work of thy fingers, the moon, and the stars, which you have set in place, what is mankind that t you are mindful of them, human beings that you care for them" (Psalm 8:3-6, NIV).

Infidelity brings a flood of negative emotions that can create significant stress. Imagine how transformative it could be to intentionally incorporate positive emotions into your life. Like David of old, amid the negative experiences of infidelity, take some time to look up into the heavens and view in awe the grandeur of the stars. Worship the One who created such beauty. In this emotionally challenging time, be reminded that the same awesome God who holds the stars in space holds you in the palm of His hand and has promised that He will never leave or forsake you!

> *"Positive emotions are not trivial luxuries, but instead might be critical necessities for optimal functioning."*
>
> -BARBARA FREDRICKSON

INCORPORATE THE POSTIVE EMOTION OF HOPE

There is a list of emotions that you might consider incorporating into your life as you navigate the challenging path of infidelity, but perhaps the most significant during this season is **hope.** Robert Schuller wisely stated, "Let your hopes, not your hurts, shape your future."[128]

Merriam-Webster defines *hope* as both a verb and a noun. As a verb, it means, "to cherish a desire with anticipation: to want something to happen or be true."[129] As a noun, it means, "a desire by expectation of or belief in fulfillment."[130] J.R. Beck viewed hope as partly cognitive (a thought), emotional (an anticipation), and volitional (a belief), and traditionally has been linked with a religious or spiritual connotation.[131] The American Psychological Association (APA) defines hope as "the expectation that positive experiences will occur, or that a negative situation will not materialize or will result in a favorable outcome."[132]

STEPS OF PSYCHOLOGICAL HEALING

TAKE TIME FOR REFLECTION

Only the person who has endured sexual or emotional infidelity truly knows the emotional pain associated it brings. The innocent party's mind often becomes a dumping ground for a torrent of negative and destructive thoughts. Rona B. Subotnik and Gloria G. Harris, in their book *Surviving Infidelity,* stated that "negative thoughts may have negative themes"[133] and listed four inaccurate themes identified by Dr. Aaron Beck, founder of cognitive therapy. These themes may easily be applied by individuals navigating infidelity. They are:

- Negative Opinion of Yourself
- Self-Blame
- Negative Interpretation of Events
- Negative Expectations of the Future[134]

A healthy approach to addressing emotional pain is to intentionally reflect on both positive thoughts and the admirable characteristics of the offending spouse. Consider, for example, the traits that initially drew you to your spouse. What were the outstanding positive qualities that captivated you? What fun activities did you enjoy together? Reflect on the emotions you experienced during your first date. What struggles did you face as a couple, and what victories did you celebrate together?

Having identified multiple positive reflections, turn your thoughts toward the possibility of forgiveness and reconciliation. Recognize that, together, you can start over, recommitting in your heart to your spouse and embracing the challenges of restoration and healing as a unified team.

DISMISS UNWANTED THOUGHTS

As you move forward, becoming mentally and psychologically healthy, you may find yourself recalling fond memories from your marriage—holidays, vacations, picnics, the birth of your children, and cherished family times together. You may also reflect on the challenges and struggles you faced together. However, the most difficult thoughts you may face are those surrounding the horrific betrayal.

As human beings, we often suppress negative thoughts to cope, but is there a more constructive and effective way to address them? I believe there is. We find it in the Apostle Paul's exhortation to the Philippians where he wrote, "Finally, brothers, whatever is true, whatever is noble, whatever is right, whatever is pure, whatever is lovely, whatever is admirable—if anything is excellent or praiseworthy—think about such things" (Philippians 3:8, NIV). How we think is so important.

As human beings, we exhibit behavior that flows from our instincts. For example, it is natural for us to desire food, water, shelter, relationships (community), procreation, and caring for our biological offspring. However, we are the only created beings on earth that can consciously think. No wonder Paul exhorted us to "think" admirable and noble thoughts. This is something we can do!

A.W. Tozer saw the results of thinking and wrote, "Thinking stirs feelings, and feelings triggers actions."[135]

Do you think the Apostle Paul may have understood that we cannot think two thoughts at the same time? Scientifically, a person can't think two distinct thoughts simultaneously. Our brains can only process one thought at a time. Psychological research shows that our mental "central executive" is amazingly limited—we can only process one thought at a time, at a meager rate of five or ten per second at most.[136] You've likely heard the term "multitasking," which is probably more correct as "multi-sequencing." Our brains can rapidly switch between thoughts, but they cannot think of two thoughts simultaneously. This insight allows us to acknowledge negative intrusive thoughts and intentionally redirect our focus to good thoughts. David illustrates this when he declared, "When I am afraid, I will trust in you" (Psalm 56:3, NIV).

The point is that, rather than trying to suppress our thoughts, we can redirect them or deal with unwanted intrusive thoughts by replacing them with healthy, constructive ones. Gordon Fee, commenting on Philippians 4:8, noted that in this verse, the Apostle Paul is calling on the Philippians "one final time to 'give their minds' to nobler things."[137]

What better way to shift to healthy thoughts than by quoting the Word of God? Like David, we can hide God's Word in our hearts—memorizing it so that it becomes our default mechanism for escaping the tyranny of intrusive thoughts. While this may take some time, the more we exercise the process, the better we may become at using Scripture as our refuge and guide.

DISMISS NEGATIVE THOUGHTS

Not only are there intrusive, unwanted thoughts, but as there are also negative opinions you may have formed about yourself. As we stated in chapter one, "The innocent must be aware of the danger of self-blame founded upon false perceptions of his or her inadequacies." Such negative, false perceptions or thoughts, when entertained, can be destructive and contribute to prolonging your suffering. It is crucial to take time to identify your negative thoughts.

This principle can also apply to the guilty partner. While they know they have violated the trust and committed adultery, one horrific act of betrayal does not erase the good qualities they may possess. Focusing solely on the negative act of betrayal diminishes the broader scope of their character and potential for growth and redemption.

Referencing the innocent party of the sexual betrayal, it is essential to understand how powerful negative self-perceptions can be. Dr. Kevin Skinner, in his book *Treating Trauma from Sexual Betrayal,* listed five negative self-beliefs reported by the innocent party:

- 78% felt their partner acted out because they were not good enough.
- 62 % believed it was their fault their partner sexually acted out

- 84% felt ashamed because of their partner's actions.
- 41% thought they were a bad person because of their partner's behavior.
- 74% felt different from everyone else since discovering their partner's betrayal.[138]

DISMISS DENIAL

The APA Dictionary of Psychology defines denial as "A defense mechanism in which unpleasant thoughts, feelings, wishes, or events are ignored or excluded from conscious awareness. It may take such forms as refusal to acknowledge the reality of a terminal illness, financial problem, substance use or other addiction, or partner's infidelity. Denial is an unconscious process that functions to resolve emotional conflict or reduce anxiety. Also called disavowal."[139]

Denial is often employed by both the innocent and the guilty spouse as a psychological process, as a defensive mechanism to avoid imminent confrontation, painful realities, or potential loss. Bruce Fisher and Robert Altberti, in their book *Rebuilding Where Relationships End*, viewed denial as an "emotional safety valve," further explaining that the body will endeavor to "compensate" when faced with physical pain.[140]

Both spouses, in their ways, seek to navigate a dilemma before them. The guilty spouse may wrestle with the decision of whether to admit to the infidelity, fearing their spouse might abandon the marriage. Similarly, the innocent spouse may hesitate to confront the betraying partner, worrying that the confrontation could drive them further into the arms of their lover.

Dr. James Dobson explained that the psychological process of denial "is designed to protect the mind from an unacceptable thought or reality."[141] Marriage and family therapist Rona B. Subotnik wrote that denial "is not purposeful, but an unconscious process that protects us from unbearable pain."[142] Though this may be true, sooner or later, individuals must confront the revealed truth for healing to begin.

In the context of infidelity, even if reconciliation does not take place, confronting and processing the truth allows time to face the pain, acknowledge it, and work toward becoming emotionally, physically, psychologically, and spiritually healthy to move forward in life.

Melody Beattie, in her book *Codependent No More*, references Claudia L. Jewett's work, *Helping Children Cope with Separation and Loss*, where Jewett explores the concept of denial. Summarizing some of Jewett's observations on how people react to loss, Beattie wrote: "Reactions typical of denial include: refusing to believe reality (No, this can't be!); denying of minimizing the importance of the loss ("It's no big deal"); denying any feelings about the loss ("I don't care"); or mental avoidance (obsessing, compulsive behaviors, and keeping busy)."[143]

Protecting oneself through denial rather than confronting a painful truth is a hard road to travel. A powerful example can be found in Jesus Christ's conversation with a woman at a well. Jesus addressed a difficult circumstance in her life. When He said, "Go call your husband and come here," the woman answered Him, declaring that she had 'no husband.' Jesus replied, "You are right in saying, I have no husband: for you have had five husbands, and the one you now have is not your husband. What you said is true" (John 4:16-19). By confronting the truth, her life was radically changed.

Melody Beattie, in her book *Codependent No More*, wrote, "Denial is the shock absorber for the soul. It is an instinctive and natural reaction to pain loss, and change. It protects us. It wards off the blows of life until we can gather our other coping resources."[144]

DEVELOPING ACTIVE LISTENING

What is active listening, and how can it help heal the wounded and broken heart of a spouse who has suffered the painful betrayal of sexual or emotional infidelity? Active listening involves intentionally focusing on the act of listening, with the goal of truly hearing the other person.

Have you ever spoken to someone who seemed miles away, leaving you feeling unheard or dismissed? Active listening seeks to eliminate that experience by creating an environment where the speaker feels safe to share their thoughts and emotions without fear of interruption, cross-examination, or condemnation.

Active listening is about hearing not only words being spoken but also understanding the emotions and intentions behind them. It involves resisting the urge to immediately formulate a reply or rush into judgment. Instead, it encourages patience, making room for the speaker to fully express themselves. This form of listening is characterized by attentiveness, such as maintaining eye contact, and demonstrating a genuine effort to understand the speaker's perspective, position, and thought processes.

Where physical or emotional betrayal has occurred in a relationship, active listening plays a critical role in fostering good communication, which is essential for reconciling the marriage. By actively listening, each spouse demonstrates a sense of value and respect for the other, regardless of whether what is being said is perceived as correct or incorrect, right or wrong.

ENGAGE IN CONFRONTATION

Confronting a spouse, you suspect or know is having an adulterous affair is perhaps one of the most difficult tasks that you will ever undertake. However, refusing to address such betrayal is like ignoring a malignant tumor. As the saying goes, "You can't change what you refuse to confront."[145] Dr. James Dobson, in his book *Love Must Be Tough*, wrote, "Just as a rebellious preschooler can profit from a well-timed spanking, the psychological consequences of sinful behavior should be experienced by the guilty."[146]

Spouses should not shrink from confrontation when it becomes necessary. Adultery necessitates that the innocent spouse confronts the betraying spouse. Though painful and difficult, confrontation can provide psychological relief by bringing truth to light. Once the reality is faced, the marriage now has the potential to be repaired, reconciled, and ultimately restored.

Rather than confront a cheating spouse, the innocent spouse may resort to the philosophical concept of unconditional love. However, unconditional love in a marriage—especially in the face of infidelity—should not be misconstrued as overlooking the betrayal, being passive, or refusing to rock the boat. Unconditional love means addressing the issue of infidelity, exposing it as a sinful betrayal, and demonstrating a willingness to forgive one's spouse while actively seeking reconciliation.

ENGAGE IN PRAYER

Prayer can be seen as both a psychological and spiritual step in healing from the pain of sexual infidelity, benefiting both the innocent and the offending spouse. Psychologically, prayer offers a way for a spouse to take control over the adverse circumstances surrounding infidelity. Instead of resorting to self-pity and isolation—which can lead to depression—the hurting spouse focuses their attention on a positive course of action. What can be more positive, uplifting, comforting, and life-changing than communicating with God in prayer? C.D. Dolph wrote that when people pray, they are communicating with God. This act of communication impacts their circumstances and lives, increases the sense of mastery, lowers stress, and promotes a sense of self-efficacy. These effects are linked to a decrease in anxiety and depression while improving one's ability to perform a variety of tasks.[147] In addition, he wrote:

> Prayer serves important cognitive purposes. Praying is a means of controlling or ordering one's thoughts which may in itself reduce anxiety that comes from racing thoughts and feeling out of control. Prayer may be a type of cognitive therapy in which people review their attributions, set their expectations and rehearse their beliefs.[148]

STEPS OF SPIRITUAL HEALING

INCORPORATE CONFESSION

Confession is a crucial step in the process of spiritual healing, applicable to both Christians and non-Christians. It is difficult because the sinful nature of humanity instinctively seeks to defend, deny, hide, and rationalize wrongdoing, all while carrying the unbearable weight of shame and guilt. This internal struggle is compounded by fear, anxiety, insecurity, uncertainty, and the potential for scorn or rejection. From a biblical worldview that acknowledges "All have sinned and come short of the glory of God" (Romans 3:20, KJV), it becomes evident that it is not merely the sins themselves but the inherently fallen nature of humanity that makes confession so challenging. Jesus declared this truth when He said, "For out of the heart proceed evil thoughts murders, adulteries, fornications, thefts, false witness, blasphemies" (Matthew 15:19, KJV).

Confession, in this context, is offered by the offending spouse as a heartfelt acknowledgment of the sin they have committed, which has been weighing heavily on their heart and mind or, as some describe, "on their conscience." This confession is accompanied by genuine contrition as the individual voices their offense before God. In the same manner, confession is also directed toward the spouse who has been wronged, acknowledging the sin committed against them. It is not uncommon to hear an offending spouse express relief after confessing, saying, "I feel so much better; I'm glad I got it (the offense) off my chest." Such confession often leads to repentance and creates an opportunity for reconciliation and healing in the relationship.

INCORPORATE FORGIVENESS

Paul's command in Ephesians 4:-32 (ESV), " Be kind to one another, tenderhearted, forgiving one another, as God in Christ forgave you" stands in stark contrast to the law given by Moses in Leviticus 24:1-20 (ESV), which states, "If anyone injures his neighbor, as he has done it shall be done to him, fracture for fracture, eye for eye, tooth for tooth; whatever injury he has given a person shall be given to him." As the world population in 2025 edges toward 8.2 billion people, imagine if we were still living under the Levitical law. The demand for optometrists, ophthalmologists, dentists, oral surgeons, and orthopedic surgeons would be overwhelming, making these professions among the most lucrative. Without such professionals, the world would be filled with toothless smiles, disfigured faces, and distorted limbs.

A meaningful definition of forgiveness is found in the *Baker Encyclopedia of Psychology & Counseling,* which describes it as "the overcoming of negative thoughts, feelings, and behaviors not by denying the offense or the right to be hurt or angry but viewing the offender with acceptance (if not compassion) so that the forgiver can be healed."[149]

Forgiveness is a conscious and deliberate act of the will. In the Lord's masterful parable of the unforgiving servant, Jesus taught that each one of us has the choice to forgive and that true forgiveness demonstrates a heart of compassion. Note carefully the Lord's words to the unforgiving servant:

> Then his master, after he had called him, said to him, 'You wicked servant I forgave you all the debt because you begged me. 'Should you have had compassion on your servant, just as I had pity on you? And his master was angry, and delivered him to the torturers until he should pay all that was due to him. So My heavenly Father also will do to you if each of you, from his heart, does not forgive his brother his trespasses. (Matthews 18:32-35).

If forgiveness is a conscious and deliberate act of the will, combined with a heart of compassion, it must also be understood as a continuous process. True forgiveness is unlikely to occur instantly. Instead, it unfolds progressively as an ongoing inward choice to forgive, paired with consistent outward expressions of that forgiveness. This process ultimately leads to the heartfelt declaration, "I have forgiven you."

Having sat with many couples navigating the challenging process of restoring trust in their marriage while processing their emotions and thoughts, I have observed that marriages beginning to heal share a common denominator: the willingness to forgive. An oft-repeated truth is that forgiveness not only frees the offender but also the liberates the person who was offended. Imagine heading toward a door and noticing a person with his hands full is struggling to open the same door you are about to enter. You react and say, "Let me open the door for you." Forgiveness is like this. When you choose to forgive the person who offended you, you open the door of healing for their struggling heart, while simultaneously opening the same door to your healing.

When we consider physical or sexual infidelity, the offender often struggles with accepting that God would forgive them, forgiving themselves, and navigating the emotional process of receiving forgiveness from the innocent party. Forgiveness serves as a powerful healing balm, easing stress, anxiety, and depression. It is not merely a noble act but a vital process for personal well-being. Dr. Khoddam aptly stated, "By letting go of anger and resentment, we create a healthier emotional environment within ourselves. Cultivating forgiveness practices can significantly impact our mental health and emotional healing."[150]

Lewis Smedes, in his book *Forgive and Forget,* provides a solid common-sense approach to forgiveness. He emphasizes that forgiveness does not mean tolerating wrongful actions, stating that you may forgive someone but still "refuse to tolerate what they have done."[151] Thomas Fuller captured the importance of forgiveness, both giving and receiving, when he wrote, "He that cannot forgive others breaks the bridge over which he must pass himself; for every man has need to be forgiven."[152]

Honest and sincere forgiveness is essential for healing. Without forgiveness, healing, reconciliation. and the renewal of passion, intimacy, and commitment becomes as absurd as playing the piano without fingers. Forgiveness allows the shadow of shame to lift, making way for the sunshine of hope to break through. Cindy Belle wrote, "Our journey to trust and forgive people who have betrayed us begins with trusting God."[153]

Martin Luther King Jr. so eloquently stated, "Forgiveness does not mean ignoring what has been done or putting a false label on an evil act. It means, rather, that the evil act no longer remains as a barrier to the relationship."[154]

Perhaps the greatest struggle in forgiving a spouse for infidelity is the recurring intrusion of memories that disrupt daily life, requiring you to forgive them again. Deliverance from thoughts of bitterness or anger comes through deliberate expression, "I remember, but I remember it forgiven." This affirmation not only disarms the intrusive thoughts but also extinguishes the fiery darts of bitterness and anger that the enemy of our souls would nefariously seek to exploit. It fosters a continual attitude of intentional and decisive forgiveness.

When a couple is navigating the bitter experience of sexual infidelity, much emphasis is placed upon the innocent spouse forgiving the guilty spouse. However, there may be instances where the innocent spouse needs to seek forgiveness for holding resentment or anger toward themselves—commonly called self-blame. Forgiving oneself is an essential act of healthy self-care.

Having defined forgiveness, it is equally important to consider what forgiveness is not. The journey to forgive a spouse for sexual infidelity can be arduous if misconceptions about forgiveness create barriers and inhibit progress.

Forgiveness is not a deliberate or unquestionable approval of the offense.

Some people mistakenly believe that forgiving their spouse implies approving or condoning their actions. This misconception unfairly shifts the emphasis onto the innocent party, as if they are the ones being judged. However, the wrong choices your spouse made are not a reflection of you, and you are not on trial. Did Christ approve of the unjust treatment He endured during His trial and crucifixion? No, but he was still willing to forgive those responsible.

Forgiveness is not canceling the consequences of the offense.

Sexual betrayal will always have consequences. For example, the emotional turmoil of sexual betrayal is so intense and unbearable that the offending party is asked to leave the home. This action can create financial challenges, such as restructuring bank accounts to ensure financial survival. While these measures may be difficult for the offending spouse, they are a direct result of their actions. The innocent spouse is not obligated to release or pardon their spouse of such costs and consequences. The offending party is not off the hook, excused, or excluded from the consequences of their choice.

Forgiveness is not denying the act of sexual betrayal.

For the innocent party processing the act of sexual betrayal, denying the offense is as ludicrous as denying the sweetness of sugar and the bitterness of vinegar. This hypocritical act often takes place when the innocent spouse endeavors to maintain peace at all costs. It is a presumptuous and precarious act, creating a false narrative to friends, family, and the community. It is entirely natural for the innocent spouse to not only feel hurt but also to experience righteous anger toward the sin of adultery.

Forgiveness is not minimizing the severity of the sexual act of betrayal.

As a pastor, I have sat in counseling sessions where the innocent spouse intentionally minimized the infidelity that occurred. For example, the wife might say, "My husband was drunk." However, being drunk does not dismiss his volitional choices, soothe his conscience, or serve as a panacea for reconciliation. Similarly, some spouses minimize the adulterous affair by rationalizing their actions, declaring that "so many people in society are committing adultery." How ludicrous! Comparing your infidelity with the infidelity of others is like recklessly ignoring a "BRIDGE OUT" sign simply because others are speeding ahead.

Forgiveness is not the total abandoning of past or future feelings.

When God created you, He created you with a soul that is comprised of intellect, will, and emotions. When you forgive, all three of these components are actively at work. However, the emotional aspect of forgiveness often requires continual processing. The more severe the wound, the longer the time needed to process the emotions. Typically, the volitional and intellectual decisions to forgive usually precede the emotional processing.

As a spouse moves forward in the emotional process, there may be incidents in the future that trigger painful reminders of the betrayal. For example, if a spouse is caught red-handed flirting with someone of the opposite sex, those painful feelings can immediately resurface. It's as if the wound that has been progressively healing is suddenly ripped open again.

During a war, battles often end with the raising of a white flag, signifying total surrender of the opposing enemy. Once the battle is over, the white flag is accepted and discarded. However, when it comes to sexual or emotional infidelity, the metaphorical "white flag of feelings" is never completely relinquished. Battles with emotions may still arise, even as healing has occurred and continues to progress.

The innocent spouse may find themselves processing lingering emotions linked to past betrayals, especially when future incidents provoke unhealthy emotional reactions involving a spouse and the opposite sex. Unlike past instances of denial, lying, and secrecy, any emotional indiscretion is now swiftly confronted. Boundaries are instantly and emphatically discussed and implemented, ensuring that the marriage covenant remains protected and further rifts are prevented.

Forgiveness is not assuming that reconciliation will take place with your spouse.

It is the goal of Christian counseling that a spouse honestly forgives their partner when infidelity has occurred in a marriage. Reconciliation is the goal. However, while forgiveness is an act within your control, reconciliation is not. Reconciliation requires the mutual agreement and effort of both spouses, making it an arrangement that cannot be achieved by the will of only one. Forgiveness, in essence, is an individual act, while reconciliation is a partnership.

This reality can be likened to the operation of a seesaw, which requires the participation of two individuals to function. Without the willingness of both parties, reconciliation in a marriage covenant becomes as unattainable as the up-and-down motion of a seesaw with only one person. Shirley P. Glass, in her book *Not "Just Friends,"* highlighted this challenge, noting that reconciliation becomes impossible when the spouse less committed to the marriage is determined to leave, despite the heroic effort of the committed partner.[155]

We must understand that Jesus permitted the innocent party to divorce their spouse due to sexual infidelity. At the same time, we must also recognize that God hates divorce and that if reconciliation is possible and desired, it is often the better course of action. The concept of reconciliation for a betrayed spouse is deeply rooted in the biblical concept of reconciliation, exemplified in Christ who freely and volitionally provided forgiveness and reconciliation for all of broken humanity.

Paul beautifully wrote, "So, as those who have been chosen of God, holy and beloved, put on the heart of compassion, kindness, humility, gentleness, and patience, bearing with one another, and forgiving each other, whoever has a complaint against anyone; just as the Lord forgave you, so also should you" (Colossians 3:12-13, NASB). Christ's payment for the sins of humanity was sufficient. If his payment for the sins of humanity was enough, is not the grace of God, the blood of Christ, and reconciliation sufficient for you to forgive your spouse?

Forgiveness is not forgetting the sexual betrayal.

The offending spouse may quickly say, "You need to forgive and forget." This flawed reasoning fails to properly understand the progressive nature of emotional process of healing. Furthermore, it disregards the brain's natural ability to remember both negative and positive events and circumstances. In today's advanced technological era, a single keystroke can erase entire pages of data on a computer by hitting the "delete" button. However, the human brain does not function like that—it does not effortlessly "delete" painful, embarrassing, bitter, or traumatic memories. Instead, it works tirelessly to remember them.

During a pastoral counseling session at Zion City in Tucson, Arizona, Senior Pastor Waylon Sears shared one of the best solutions addressing the challenge of remembering offenses while offering forgiveness. While affirming the fact we do remember negative offenses and our minds do not instantaneously go blank, he provided an enlightening and comforting process in which the offended party may sincerely say, "I remember, but I remember it forgiven!"

What a powerful declaration! This mindset thwarts revenge, suffocates anger, hushes hate, terminates bitterness, reduces anxiety, instills hope, ushers in peace, demonstrates humility, reflects unconditional love, and silently offers reconciliation.

Remembering the offense is not necessarily a bad thing. In fact, it can provide instant opportunities to learn from the past by judiciously identifying the terrible mistakes that were made in the marriage. These memories can act as "guardrails" that help protect the relationship from potential emotional pain and anguish in the future.

Michele Weiner-Davis, reflecting on her work with individuals who experienced sexual betrayal, shared an insightful observation about memories. She wrote,

"Memories of the affair begin to occur less and less frequently. And when they do happen, the intensity with which people experience emotions tends to shift dramatically over time."[156]

In Christian circles, much emphasis is placed on the necessity of forgiving the offending spouse, but caution must be exercised to avoid forgiving too soon. Premature forgiveness, offered without uncovering the whole truth or allowing time for the offended spouse to process their emotions, may send the wrong message—that forgiveness is easy. This could, in turn, open the door for future acts of infidelity by the same spouse. Forgiveness given hastily might bypass the uncomfortable yet essential process of addressing deep emotions and unresolved issues. It may fail to account for the whole person—spiritually, emotionally, psychologically, and socially.

Through counseling, I have encountered married couples where infidelity occurred not only once, but twice, and in some cases, three times. Infidelity is far more than just a "hiccup in the relationship," "a bump in the road," or just "a slip-up." It represents a serious breach in a relationship's trust and commitment. As such, it demands careful emotionally processing and mature, honest discussions to ensure it is not dismissed superficially or treated lightly.

Forgiveness is not a feeling.

As previously stated, emotional hurt must be processed, and the greater the hurt, the longer the process takes. However, it's important to remember that forgiveness is not a feeling. When you forgive your spouse for their infidelity, you are making a conscious choice. It is an act of your will. Corrie Ten Boom famously wrote, "Forgiveness is an act of the will, and the will can function regardless of the temperature of the heart."[157] —Corrie Ten Boom

Forgiveness is not declaring, "I trust you."

In some cases, a betrayed spouse may volitionally forgive their partner but remain hesitant to pursue reconciliation due to a lack of trust. Many circumstances may influence the inability to trust: How long has the infidelity been going on? Was the betrayal with someone close, such as a best friend or even a a sibling of the innocent spouse? Is this the first time infidelity has occurred?

PRACTICE LOVING YOURSELF

Jesus spoke candidly about loving our neighbor as we love ourselves. In this short mandate, Jesus expressed a self-love congruent with our identity—a person of infinite worth created in the image of God. When individuals involved in sexual infidelity receive forgiveness from his or her spouse, they must also forgive themselves and embrace a spiritually healthy form of self-love.

One could very easily go through life forfeiting the healthy process of self-love, but in all reality, true healing is deeply connected to this practice. Dr. Kevin Skinner expressed that "self-compassion is a requirement for true healing."[158]

Jesus' statement, "You shall know the truth, and the truth will set you free" (NKJV, 8:32), is profoundly applicable here. Experiencing spiritual wholeness and healthy self-love begins with acknowledging and living in the truth of God's Word. When you accept what the Word of God declares about your identity, you open yourself to the dynamic healing that flows from a genuine declaration of self-love. But notice the condition that precedes this awesome declaration of Jesus. He addressed the Jews who believed in Him saying, "If you abide in My Word, you are my disciples indeed" (John 8:31, NKJV).

David's heartfelt cry in Psalm 51:7 (NKJV) reflects this truth: "Purge me with hyssop and I shall be clean; Wash me and I shall be whiter than snow." Through genuine repentance, accompanied by a broken and contrite spirit, David humbly experienced the cleansing power of God. This humility allowed him to joyfully proclaim the removal of his sin, and he knew his soul had been made pure—"whiter than snow."

INCORPORATE GIVING THANKS

As hard as it may be, in perhaps one of the most difficult times in your life—facing the devastating news of your spouse's infidelity and striving to heal from this profound betrayal of trust—I encourage you to incorporate a spirit of thanksgiving in your life. The Apostle Paul exhorts believers, "In everything give thanks: for this is the will of God in Christ Jesus concerning you" (I Thessalonians 5;18, KJV).

Notice that Paul does not exhort Christians to give thanks *for everything* but rather *in everything*. Contentment is not found in the crisis but in Christ.

This verse admonishes us that in whatever circumstance we find ourselves, we can look to our heavenly Father and acknowledge He is in control of the situation. However, it is not a situation in which you are finding great comfort or pleasure. You can be thankful for his grace that is sufficient to sustain you. You can thank God that He has promised never to leave you or forsake you. Your situation or circumstances did not come as a surprise to an Omniscient God.

The Apostle Paul also exhorted the Philippian Christians to: "Do all things without murmuring and disputing, that you may become blameless and harmless, children of God without fault in the midst of a crooked and perverse generation, among whom you shine as lights in the world…" (Philippians 2:14-15, NKJV). Gratitude is a spiritual mindset that speaks of Christian maturity. Living a life of thanksgiving reflects to the world the light and life we have found in Christ Jesus.

The Apostle Paul also exhorted the Philippian Christians, "Be anxious for nothing; but in everything by pray and supplication with thanksgiving let your request be made known to God. And the peace of God, which passeth all understanding, shall keep your hearts and minds through Christ Jesus" (Philippians 4: 6-7, KJV). Billy Graham, commenting on this verse, once wrote, "A psychiatrist was quoted in a newspaper as saying that he could not improve on the Apostle Paul's prescription for human worry."[159]

Developing an attitude of gratitude not only enriches our spiritual lives but also brings benefits to other areas of our well-being. Amy Morin, a licensed clinical social worker, wrote an insightful article in *Psychology Today* entitled *7 Scientifically Benefits of Gratitude*.[160] I encourage you to read the full article, but here are the seven benefits she highlights:

- Gratitude opens the door to more relationships.
- Gratitude improves physical health.
- Gratitude improves psychological health.
- Gratitude enhances empathy and reduces aggression.
- Gratitude helps people sleep better.
- Gratitude improves self-esteem.
- Gratitude increases mental strength.

Infidelity is an incredibly difficult and heartbreaking experience for anyone to navigate. However, while information provides guidance, the true path to transformation lies in applying what we learn. During the process of spiritual healing from sexual betrayal, take some time to reflect on the things in your life for which you are thankful.

Throughout the day, try to express gratitude and thanksgiving with short prayers. As a young pastor, I once overheard an older pastor who paused at a water fountain and quietly said, "Lord, thank you for this water." He didn't realize anyone was nearby, but his short prayer inspired me to practice gratitude throughout my day, even for the little things in life.

INCORPORATE PRAYER

When your heart is healing from the emotional pain of sexual infidelity, when you are physically exhausted, when reconciliation in your marriage feels impossible, and when prayer seems like an overwhelming task, making the effort to pray can bring great comfort and healing. The powerful dynamics of prayer fill the heart with hope when the primary objective of biblical prayer is connecting with God, rather than simply repeating rote phrases or overused expressions.

Experiencing the manifest presence of God in prayer not only changes life's circumstances but also transforms the person praying. Consider the story of Hagar when she found herself deserted in a desert, facing the seemingly inevitable death of her son Ishmael. She wept, and God intervened, declaring that He had heard the voice of her son (perhaps crying and praying). God opened Hagar's eyes to see a well of water, allowing her to fill her water bottle and receive a prophetic promise that Ishmael would become the father of a great nation (Genesis 21:15-21, ESV). When a person experiences God in their life, defeat is turned into victory.

Jesus succinctly stated, "When you pray" (Matthew 6:6, KJV). A.W. Tozer offered a profound insight on the power of prayer:

> Whatever God can do faith can do, and whatever faith can do prayer can do when it is offered in faith. An invitation to prayer is, therefore, an invitation to omnipotence, for prayer, engages the omnipotent God and brings Him into our human affairs. Nothing is impossible to the man who prays in faith, just as nothing is impossible with God.[161]

INCORPORATE READING THE WORD OF GOD

Jesus said, "Man shall not live by bread alone but by every word that proceedeth out of the mouth of God" (Matthew 4:4, KJV). God gave us His Word so that we may understand who He is and recognize our accountability to Him. By reading the Word of God, we derive an understanding of God's character. This understanding is essential, as it helps us to embrace the promises revealed in Scripture.

Why is this so important? As human beings, we are born with a sinful nature and cannot truly know God without His grace and the illumination of the Word by the Holy Spirit. Have you ever spent hours assembling a puzzle only to discover that one piece is missing? That "one missing piece" prevents us from fully appreciating the beauty the designer intended. Similarly, the Word of God provides humanity with the missing pieces of knowledge, revealing the purpose of our existence and allowing us to enjoy life as God intended.

When we experience being "born again," we discover what Jesus taught Nicodemus in John chapter three. We are like babies who need spiritual nourishment from the Word of God to grow in grace, deepen our knowledge of Him, and see the promises fulfilled in our lives.

Christians navigating the emotional, physical, social, psychological, and spiritual challenges caused by the horrific rift of sexual infidelity in their marriage need the spiritual bread Jesus referred to for sustenance. They find hope and strength in the promises of God's Word. Why is this? Because the promises of God are rooted in His unchanging character. When a Christian discovers God's character through His Word, they can trust Him—knowing that He is faithful, unchanging, and incapable of lying. They are assured that God will never leave or fail them and will work through all the adverse circumstances for their ultimate good.

STEPS FOR PHYSICAL HEALING

We learned in chapter one that stress is a significant factor when navigating the emotional turmoil of sexual infidelity. Stress can have both minor and major impacts on your physical body. It is important to recognize the potential benefits of gratitude in managing stress. As research suggests, "People who are grateful feel less pain, less stress, suffer insomnia less, have stronger immune systems, experience healthier relationships, and do better academically and professionally. Overall, it can boost your mental and spiritual health."[162] How can you reduce stress? Here are some suggestions to consider.

AVOID ALCOHOL AND HARMFUL DRUGS

When struggling with emotional or physical pain, people often turn to default coping mechanisms. One common but unwise choice is relying on alcohol or drugs. However, these substances never improve the situation or relieve the pain. You can't drown your sorrows or eliminate stress with alcohol. As a depressant, alcohol not only fails to address the root cause of stress but also distorts the unique personality God gave you. Instead, it's important to seek healthier, more constructive ways to cope with stress.

It is common knowledge that alcohol destroys brain cells. Dr. Pierce J. Howard noted that alcohol primarily affects the "left hemisphere of the brain," and heavy drinkers kill approximately "60,000 more neurons a day" in contrast to light drinkers. Over time, this damage is substantial, as the brains of heavy drinkers upon death weigh "105 grams less" than that of light drinkers at the time of death.

Drugs, as you likely know, can lead to a dangerous path of addiction. In 2022, the Diagnostic and Statistical Manual of Mental Disorders (DSM-5) reported that 24 million people aged 12 and over met the criteria for substance abuse disorder.[163] This alarming statistic clearly highlights the risks of turning to drugs as a coping mechanism for stress.

SLEEP

During my time interning with Dr. James Abanishe, a Christian Psychiatrist at Mountain Dew Behavioral Health, while pursuing my Master of Arts Degree in Pastoral Counseling: Marriage and Family, we had a meaningful conversation about the importance of sleep. He explained that if a person were to live for 90 years and sleep 8 hours a night, they would have spent 30 years of their life sleeping.

Dallis Willard, in his book *Renovation of the Heart,* highlighted the value of sleep in relation to trust in God. Commenting on the Sabbath, he stated, "Sleep is a good first use of solitude and silence. It is also a good indicator of how thoroughly we trust God." He pointed to the example of David, who, despite experiencing danger and uncertainly, slept well because of his faith in God's protection.

David's trust is evident in Psalm 3:5: "I lay down and slept: I awoke, for the Lord sustains me." Similarly, in Psalm 4:8, David proclaimed, "In peace I will both lie down and sleep for You alone, O Lord, make me to dwell in safety."[164]

We can easily see the importance of sleep and the wisdom of God in creating night and day. Sleep allows your body to rejuvenate and refresh itself. When you are well-rested, you will notice greater clarity in your thinking. However, when a person is stressed, sleep can become elusive and difficult to achieve.

Melatonin, a hormone naturally produced in your body, plays a key role in promoting sleep. It is produced during the dark hours of the night and decreases with exposure to daylight. To maximize your body's natural melatonin production, create a dark environment in your bedroom by using blackout curtains or minimizing artificial light. If you are still struggling with sleep, talk to your doctor about taking a melatonin supplement to help you feel strengthened and refreshed each day.

An adage suggests, "Drink some warm milk before going to sleep," and it remains as a good practice. Warm milk metabolizes quicker in your body than cold milk, helping promote relaxation and sleep. Dr. Pierce J. Howard wrote, "Milk products stimulate melatonin production, which improves sleep. Whether skim of fat, milk (like complex carbohydrates) contain *L-tryptophan,* the amino acid that is a precursor of melatonin (and serotonin)."[165]

EXERCISE

Engaging in regular exercise is another vital practice for reducing stress and improving overall well-being. There are many different forms of exercise to choose from, such as walking, running, jogging, aerobics, swimming, biking, playing different sports, weightlifting, gardening, hunting, fishing, etc. The key is finding an activity that suits your interests and capabilities.

When you exercise, the pituitary gland and hypothalamus in your brain release endorphins—neurotransmitters that help you relax, improve your mood, and relieve stress.

These endorphins are often called "happy hormones". Dr. Howard J. Pierce, highlighting the benefits of exercise, referenced Rod Dishman, a professor of exercise science at the University of Georgia. Dishman identified that "sustained exercise" leads to an increase in epinephrine levels. This elevated epinephrine "serves to lubricate the individual's mechanism for coping with stress."[166]

As beneficial as exercise is, you might want to consider the timing of your workout. Exercising right before bed may disrupt your ability to get a good night's rest. "Exercise tends to elicit cortical alertness—not what you want when going to sleep."[167] For example, if you like to jog or lift weights, engaging in these activities late at night could stimulate your nervous system, keeping it alert rather than allowing it to slow down for sleep.

PRIORITIZE

When infidelity is discovered, it is not unusual for the innocent party to feel overwhelmed, dealing with intense emotions, anxiety, and stress. It is crucial to take time to prioritize your actions. For example, a top priority may be setting aside some time to confront the offending spouse in a safe environment and affirming whether what has been revealed is true.

The next step might be for the offended spouse to take time to sort through all the pieces of information and process the emotional hurt. Afterward, the offending spouse may consider seeking individual counseling. If both spouses agree to work on the marriage, extended counseling sessions for the couple can be scheduled. However, if either spouse decides not to work on the marriage, the next step could involve consulting a lawyer. Additionally, a financial advisor might be brought into the picture to address financial concerns and plan for the future.

The next action step might involve revealing the infidelity to the children and discussing the decisions that have been made. Prioritizing tasks is key—taking one step at a time helps prevent being overwhelmed by the situation.

While prioritizing, it's also helpful to eliminate things that contribute to stress. For example, consider what tasks you're currently doing that you don't have to do. Identify things you don't enjoy but are necessary and find alternatives. For example, if your spouse previously took care of the lawn, and they are no longer in the picture, you might ask a friend to help temporarily or hire someone to take care of it. On the flip side, think about activities you enjoy that calm and rejuvenate you. This might include a favorite hobby, visiting a serene environment, or meeting with a good friend.

EAT HEALTHY

This is a no-brainer, but you might say, "I do not feel like eating!" The emotional trauma of infidelity can certainly suppress your appetite or conversely lead to overeating or consuming unhealthy food. However, maintaining a healthy diet is crucial for many areas of your life. It directly impacts your physical, emotional, psychological, and spiritual well-being. Eating nutritious food is essential to properly function and meet the demands of life, many of which may be highly stressful.

You must care for yourself to care for your children, family, and future effectively. Neglecting your health in the present makes it harder to positively sow into your future. As research shows, "Poor diets — often high in refined foods, added sugars, fried foods, and processed meats — are linked to inflammation, depression, and anxiety. In contrast, nutritious, balanced diets can help reduce risk or improve management of depression and anxiety."[168]

Dr. Pierce J. Howard suggested that a person can reduce stress in their life by cutting back on fats, sugars, smoking, and alcohol.[169] I encourage you to see your family physician, who can assist you with any physical symptoms resulting from stress. Additionally, seeking professional counseling or the guidance of a nutritionist can provide valuable support.

HUMOR

There is certainly no humor in the topic of infidelity itself. However, adding humor into your life can be very beneficial when processing the serious matter of infidelity. Authors John C. Thomas and Lisa Sosia stated that The Association for Applied and Therapeutic Humor (AATH) listed several psychological and physical benefits of humor. AATH declared that humor triggers the release of endorphins (the body's natural painkillers), stimulates the cardiovascular system, relieves stress, prevents negative tension, and helps people face life's challenges creatively.[170] Humor may be found in a funny story, a joke, or a funny movie. It can help a person avoid taking yourself too seriously. As Bugs Bunny humorously remarked, "Don't take life too seriously, people are dying to get out of it."

STEPS FOR SOCIAL HEALING

SOCIAL BOUNDARIES

Dr. Henry Cloud and Dr. John Townsend, in their book *Boundaries*, wrote, "Just as homeowners set physical property lines around their land, we need to set mental, physical emotional and spiritual boundaries for our lives to help us distinguish what is our responsibility and what isn't.[171] To their list, I would also add social boundaries.

Infidelity demands establishing new boundaries in the social world we live in, where sexual boundaries have been violated. Relationships with the opposite sex must be carefully discussed, and all contact with the third party, male or female, that led to infidelity must be completely severed. Failure to do so is like allowing a wolf into a sheep pen, where havoc and destruction are bound to occur. Opposite-sex relationships can become fertile ground for another affair to develop.

Men and women navigating the healing process can find help by confiding in individuals of the same sex who are willing to invest time, listen, and provide honest feedback.

All contact must be terminated, including phone calls, texting, and emails. Additionally, social media platforms such as Instagram, Facebook, Snap Chat, Twitter, and TikTok—which could serve as direct or indirect means of re-establishing contact with a former lover—must be abandoned. Some bridges simply need to be burned!

Any attempts to rebuild trust in the relationship will be futile if the offending spouse refuses to completely sever social connections that contributed to the infidelity.

Creating social boundaries in the workplace can be especially challenging. In some cases, the pain caused by the rift in the relationship makes it difficult for the innocent spouse to envision moving forward if social contact with the individual involved in the adulterous affair is required for work tasks. Changing jobs might be a solution, but at what cost? Is the marriage worth the sacrifice it costs?

Perhaps alternative solutions exist, such as working a different shift at the place of employment. Moving to a new geographical location and making a fresh start could also be an option. In other cases, where contact with the individual is minimal, the offending spouse may establish strong moral boundaries to ensure that no emotional flames are rekindled.

SOCIAL LIFESTYLE

If both spouses are committed to staying in the marriage, it may require changes in their social lifestyle. For example, consider the couples you hang out with—do they have a negative or positive impact on your relationship? Solomon stated, "As iron sharpens iron, so a man sharpens the countenance of his friend" (Proverbs 27:17, NKJV). The character of our friends often reveals and influences who we are.

Michele Weiner-Davis, in her book *Healing from Infidelity*, referenced a study highlighting the contagious nature of divorce. The study found that individuals were 75% more likely to divorce if they had a close friend who was divorced. Furthermore, 33% of marriages were more likely to end if they had a friend of a friend whose marriage ended in divorce.[172]

SOCIAL ATMOSPHERE

What are some places that perhaps you need to avoid to protect your marriage? Consider which vacation spots might not be conducive to building a strong relationship. Reflect on relationships that could pose a danger or become destructive in your marriage. Think about situations that might challenge your commitment to your spouse, such as working late with someone of the opposite sex, attending work-related seminars, or even doing favors for a neighbor of the opposite sex.

Ask yourself: When is hugging someone of the opposite sex not appropriate? For instance, hugging a co-worker or a stranger at a social event could potentially blur boundaries. It's also worth examining how you present yourself to others. Do you come across as flirtatious, dress inappropriately, or use overly flattering words when interacting with the opposite sex?"

SOCIAL ISOLATION

Although you are committed to staying in the marriage, you might find yourself struggling with being around people. Perhaps you wonder what others are thinking about you and find yourself isolating from society. Let me encourage you to connect with other couples, possibly through your church or community.

Psychologists and psychiatrists are still working to understand the full impact of social isolation that took place during the Covid pandemic. Dr. David Ludden, in his article *How Social Isolation Affects Intimate Couples*, wrote that even before the pandemic, research showed that socially isolated couples were more likely to vent their frustrations on each other and ultimately break up compared to couples who were well-integrated into their social networks.[173] One can easily see the significant importance of socially connecting with other couples as you navigate the challenges of moving forward in your marriage.

Dr. Reinhold Niebuhr of Union Theological Seminary in New York is credited with writing the *Serenity Prayer* (though some errantly attribute it to St. Francis of Assisi).[174] He wrote, "God grant me the serenity to accept the things I cannot change, courage to change the things I can, and the wisdom to know the difference."[175]

To move forward in the social world you live in, it is healthy to simply acknowledge and accept the infidelity that took place in your marriage while asking God to help you. While you cannot change the past, you can profoundly impact your future by having the courage to move forward and refusing to remain socially isolated.

Avoiding isolation and moving forward in your future from a social world rocked by infidelity, whether you are the offended party or the offender, is a choice only you can make. You cannot spend the rest of your life dwelling on the past or worrying about the future. Instead, you must choose to embrace the present and, with hope, anticipate a brighter future. The famous Baptist missionary to Burma, Adoniram Judson, once wrote, "The future is as bright as the promises of God."

CHAPTER 4

REBUILDING TRUST

"Rebuilding trust when it's been broken is not dependent only on the person who has broken it, or how many times they can prove they are honest. It is also about how willing you are to risk being vulnerable again." [176]

–BRENE BROWNE

Shirley Glass emphasized the critical importance of rebuilding trust in a relationship shattered by infidelity. She wrote, "Rebuilding trust is the cornerstone of the recovery process."[177] When approaching the challenge of rebuilding trust, it may helpful to begin by defining what trust truly means.

Dr. C.W. Ellison, Professor of Counseling and Urban Miniseries at Alliance Theological Seminary and Executive Director of Agape Counseling and Training Services, defined trust as, "Perceiving someone as trustworthy and placing oneself in a position of vulnerability due to the possibility of betrayal is trust."[178]

Mira Kirshenbaum defined trust as "a feeling based upon fact" and added that, most of the time, "trust is barely more than the absence of anxiety." This is a powerful statement. In marriage counseling, a client may say, "But I have a hard time trusting him/her!" It is important to examine the facts that reveal what the spouse is consistently doing to contribute positively to the relationship.

For example, consider the fact that a husband or wife is no longer texting the person with whom they were previously involved. Reflect on that fact—how does that make you feel? Does it bring a ray of hope? If trust is to be rebuilt, we must remember that feelings are often based on facts. As days, weeks, months, and years pass, and a multitude of consistent facts indicate genuine change, it becomes evident that trust is being reconstructed.

Another beautiful aspect is the understanding that trust equates to the absence of anxiety. Wow! Trust is a state where feelings are grounded in facts, and worry, fear, and anxiety no longer dominate.

Just as with processing emotions, addressing feelings, and pursuing healing, rebuilding trust within a covenant relationship is a challenging and progressive journey. The injured spouse must work hard toward trusting again, while the offending spouse must consistently demonstrate through actions over time that they can be trusted again.

However, trust is more than a matter of time, though time plays an essential role. Trust is also a matter of tactical movement. It involves how much we move towards demonstrating forgiveness, empathy, unconditional love, and grace. It is about allowing our hearts to move closer to the heart of God so that He can change us by taking away the "stony heart" and giving us a "heart of flesh".

Rebuilding trust requires moving in a new direction, adhering to principles and practices that promote growth. It means strengthening boundaries and belief systems, committing to unwavering truth and transparency, and embracing the painful yet triumphant process of transformation. It is about moving from a world filled with crushing bitterness and emotional pain to one that fosters emotional safety and security. In this space, trust grows slowly but steadily, pushing aside doubts and fears.

Trust can be compared to a triangle, with its three sides each independent of the other, coming together to form a whole. The first side of the triangle is the gift of trust, given by the innocent party to the offending party. Without this gift of trust, the process of rebuilding cannot begin. The second side is the offending party receiving and deeply valuing this trust, commiting wholeheartedly to keep and preserve it. The third side of the triangle is God, the ultimate source of strength and guidance.

Rebuilding trust is hard. How can the innocent party trust the offending party twenty-four-seven? Fear, suspicion, and nagging doubt may tend to creep into the heart of the forgiving spouse. Such fear, suspicion, and nagging doubt can be given to God. The innocent spouse releases the offending spouse into the care of an omnipresent, omniscient, and omnipotent God. The offending spouse also places the forgiving spouse into God's care, believing that they will continue to trust them without dredging up the past or harboring doubts.

Trust is a very fragile thing. It is like a once-beautiful stained-glass window that, when broken, becomes costly to repair. The offending spouse may question, "Will I ever be trusted again?" Meanwhile, the betrayed spouse questions, "How can I trust again?" "Is reconciliation even possible, and will I ever love deeply and trust fully again?"

Subotnik and Harris insightfully wrote, "The trust issue involves both of you. You want to have faith that your partner won't cheat again, and he wants to trust that you will not remind him of his betrayal for the rest of your lives."[179]

Trust is like a diamond, possessing many facets. Some facets may require additional light, careful maneuvering in the light, and clearer vision, while others are immediately seen and recognized. In this book's final segment, we will explore the various facets of the diamond of trust.

Trust is challenging. It is difficult because you must allow yourself to be vulnerable to emotional pain. It means exposing yourself to the possibility of being hurt, whether intentionally or unintentionally, because no person, no matter how nice they may be, is perfect. Trust involves facing the fear of living with a spouse who has betrayed you and wrestling with the inward question, "Will he or she be faithful to me?"

As we move into the process of rebuilding trust, the plausibility of achieving this in a marriage is unequivocally based on the alignment of your intellect, will, and emotions (soul). Your intellect must have examined the nature of the affair, considered all the psychological, sociological, and physical challenges, and acknowledged the deep emotional pain that continues to be processed. Both you and your spouse must have fully surrendered your entire will to work of rebuilding trust, understanding that there will be times when managing your emotions feels like a struggle.

Additionally, you must have fully considered and embraced the spiritual elements of faith, unconditional love, and the grace of God working within your hearts to forgive and receive forgiveness—actions that some people neither understand nor embrace. You have come to fully understand that Scripture provides the innocent spouse with the option to dissolve the marriage due to the sin of adultery (Matthew 19:9). Still, the innocent spouse has chosen, with purpose and conviction, to forgive the guilty spouse. The guilty spouse, in turn, has sincerely received both the forgiveness of the Lord and the forgiveness of their spouse.

Ultimately, trust is a progressive journey—second by second, minute by minute, hour by hour, day by day, week by week, month by month, and year by year. The journey is only completed when life on earth has concluded, and you have fulfilled your commitment to the marriage and to each other until your dying breath. Such trust points to the ability of two individuals who possessed a non-negotiable mindset, determined to do whatever it took to restore the sacred marriage covenant.

APOLOGY

Did reading the word "apology" raise your blood pressure? Have you built such an insurmountable defensive wall within your spirit that you instantly, adamantly, and quietly but resolutely said to yourself, "Never" or "Not in a thousand years." Why is an apology such a conundrum? The answer becomes clearer when approached from a theological perspective. As fallen, sinful creatures, we naturally operate from a selfish perspective, and admitting fault or offering an apology goes against our instinct to protect ourselves. The prophet Jeremiah wrote, "The heart is deceitful and desperately wicked: who can know it" (Jeremiah 17:9, KJV). In essence, it is man's pride—swallowing that pride requires humility, which is often an uncomfortable act.

Giving an honest apology is one of the greatest decisions you can make because it reflects humility, sincerity, remorse, and brokenness. It demonstrates a refusal to justify any of your actions. More than just a significant decision, it is candidly the most essential one you will make. When your spouse is navigating the deep emotional pain of betrayal, your sincere apology can become the door that allows them to begin the process of forgiveness and opens the path toward reconciling the marriage.

An apology from the spouse who has committed physical, sexual, or emotional betrayal is undoubtedly the first logical step in rebuilding trust. However, the timing of a sincere apology is critical and requires wisdom on your part. Attempting to give the right apology at the wrong time can create more havoc than healing. Remember, you are dealing with raw emotions that have intensified upon the discovery of infidelity.

Imagine walking on a narrow path in the woods, and suddenly you encounter a mother black bear with her cubs. This is not the time to continue along the path. It's time to pause, backtrack, and reassess. Similarly, while your goal of offering an apology is good, poor timing can escalate the situation. Your partner's emotions—possibly as fierce as a mother bear protecting her cubs—may not yet be ready to receive your words.

In essence, you are trying to determine the emotional state of your partner. Are they angry, shocked, overwhelmed, extremely agitated, or physically exhausted? Or are they calm, rational, and willing to talk? Demonstrating consideration for your spouse is essential, and it would be wise to inquire if it is a good time to talk. However, explicitly stating that you *want to be considerate* probably would not be wise, as consideration was notably lacking during the betrayal. Delaying the conversation does not insinuate that you are attempting to avoid giving a sincere apology.

The question often arises, "What kind of an apology do you want to hear from your spouse?" Dr. Gary Chapman wrote, "Usually the language you speak to others is the language you most want to receive."[180] Would you want your spouse to express deep regret for the betrayal, give you a word of assurance that it would never happen again, express remorse, show expressions and tears of sincerity, or candidly admit that they were wrong?

The substance of your apology must not include any phrasing that minimizes your responsibility or justifies your actions. For example, avoid statements like, "It was because you did," "I was drunk," or "You don't understand." If you find it challenging to articulate precisely what you want to say, consider writing your apology down. Then sincerely read it to your spouse. This approach can be especially beneficial if the emotional pain is still overshadowing your conversations, allowing you the opportunity to carefully select the right words.

Dr. Gary Chapman and Jennifer Thomas authored a book titled *The 5 Apology Languages: The Secret to Healthy Relationships*, where they succinctly outlined five expressions of apology that can help facilitate healing and restoration in relationships:

- Expressing regret: "I'm sorry."
- Accepting responsibility: "I was wrong."
- Making Restitution: "How can I make it right?"
- Planning for change: "I'll take steps to prevent a reoccurrence."
- Requesting forgiveness: "Can you find it in your heart to...?"[181]

TRUTH

For trust to be restored in a relationship, there must be truth. Telling the truth is often a painful and humbling experience. Shirley Glass, in her book *Not "Just Friends,"* emphasized the necessity of telling the truth to your partner. She wrote, "To cleanse the lying that occurred during the affair and in the early stages of revelation, the involved partner needs to be totally honest."[182] Miriam Webster defines trust as, "Assured reliance on the character, ability, strength, or truth of someone or something."[183]

When a partner seeks a multitude of details, the betraying partner must acquiesce and provide them, even though this is a very painful process. However, I would caution against sharing explicit sexual details. I concur with Dr. Caroline Madden, who, in her book, *After a Good Man Cheats,* pointed out that long after forgiveness has taken place and you and your spouse have moved on in the relationship, "She will think how you made love to another woman, and the specifics you gave will sabotage your physical relationship because she may not be able to forget them."[184]

The important aspect is that when the question is asked by the betrayed party, it should be truthfully answered. Lying can be more harmful and painful than an adulterous affair. For a partner to lie at any stage of questioning sabotages the entire process of reconciliation. In addition, lying only exasperates the innocent spouse. If the offending spouse does not truthfully answer one question, then why would the innocent spouse believe them when another question is asked?

Couples should be cognizant that some answers may trigger additional questions as well as deep emotions. It is important to be wise and patient, avoiding the urge to address everything at once. Focus on the main question asked and provide a sufficient answer. Revealing the truth is a highly emotional process and should be approached incrementally. Couples may benefit from setting time limits when dealing with difficult questions that demand the truth.

The innocent spouse, seeking to rebuild trust, will eventually face the reality that they must stop asking repeated questions concerning the adulterous actions of their spouse. Once the questions have been truthfully and painfully answered, forgiveness has been requested by the offending spouse and graciously given by the innocent spouse, it is time for you to begin the journey of rebuilding trust.

Cindy Beall offers good counsel for those struggling to let go of relentless questioning—often driven by curiosity—when she wrote, "Regardless of whether your marriage has survived, you must free yourself from the false need to gain more information because it will not help your journey to freedom."[185]

A marriage lacking trust cannot become a trusting one without first revealing the truth of the infidelity. From there, the process of consistently being truthful with your spouse begins, forming a cycle of trust that, like a circle, has no end.

HONESTY

What is the difference between a truthful person and an honest person? A truthful person has one predominant characteristic. Their comments are factual about any given situation with no deception involved. An honest person is not only truthful, but also upright, sincere, straightforward, fair, and actively revealing the full truth of every matter while maintaining a level of integrity, respect, and trustworthiness. Truthfulness is primarily about telling the truth. Honesty is about living the truth.

Honesty is essential for both the innocent and the offending spouse. For instance, both must be brutally honest in acknowledging that the offense has occurred—neither spouse can walk in denial. The offending spouse and the innocent spouse must also be brutally honest in their commitment to being one hundred percent invested in reconciling the marriage.

Each individual must be brutally honest in taking steps to move forward. Both must openly share their feelings and strive to understanding each other's emotions throughout the ongoing journey of reconciliation. Lastly, both must be brutally honest and willing to do whatever it takes each day to rebuild their relationship.

TRANSPARENCY

Transparency is vital in building a committed relationship. The act of sexual betrayal was covered with the dark veil of secrecy. But just as a diamond's beauty is revealed only in the light, a restored relationship is impossible without transparency. For instance, can each spouse freely pick up the other's cell phone at any time? Wow! Can you see a battle instantly forming? However, if there is nothing to hide—no questionable pictures and texts—it demonstrates a genuine effort to rebuild trust. A spouse who is not angry or defensive in such situations proves their commitment to transparency.

Solomon wisely wrote, "The wicked flee when no one pursues, but the righteous are bold as a lion" (Proverbs 28:1, KJV). If you are not hiding anything, you can boldly, confidently, and lovingly acquiesce to your spouse's request to view your cell phone.

Transparency is an ongoing process. For instance, if your former partner in the affair sends you a text, you should immediately show it to your spouse. In your spouse's presence, respond candidly to the text, making it clear that the relationship is over and firmly stating that you do not wish to see, talk to, or receive a text or email from that person. Deleting texts or emails without disclosure is not being transparent. It does not protect your spouse, especially if you have already responded to the text.

Spending money may be a big challenge in rebuilding trust. Your spouse may question your purchases, but keeping detailed receipts demonstrates your commitment to rebuilding the relationship. If the expenditure was legitimate, there is no need to be defensive. Over time, as you maintain transparency with your money, the fewer inquiries will occur. We spend money on necessities and on things we value. By valuing trust in your marriage, your transparency in spending will reveal who—and what—you truly value.

Transparency is like the crystal-clear piece of glass in an expensive window casing, allowing a spouse to see every aspect of your life. In a relationship, transparency means that your spouse has access to your passwords for electronic devices, social media accounts, bank accounts, post office boxes, calendars, your location, your circle of friends, and business associates. Does this sound extreme? Then ask yourself, "Would I have gone as far as I did in the sexual betrayal had such transparent qualities been operative in my marriage? Is the reconciliation worth embracing the transparency?

Remember, your marriage has suffered a gushing emotional wound, and being transparent in all areas of your life is a sure salve for healing the wound and restoring trust in your marriage. Transparency will eliminate even the smallest minutia of secrecy. Dr. Kathy Knickerson, in her book *Courage to Stay* wrote, "We can build trust quickly by taking some extraordinary steps to show that you have no more secrets, you mean what you say and you're doing exactly what you said you'd do."[186]

"Transparency is the currency of trust."-Freda Lewis Hall, MD

TIME

Infidelity not only produced an emotional trauma but also a directional change in trust. Trust may be diminished, deteriorated, devastated, or destroyed and it cannot be instantly or effortlessly rebuilt. The element of time is unquestionable, in that it allows a couple to methodically work in all areas of concern where trust is needed, including emotional, psychological, spiritual, and social elements. Just as a hurricane's storm surge reaches unparalleled heights and takes time to recede, the unparalleled breach of trust demands an investment of significant time and an uncompromising sincere effort.

Cindy Beall succinctly captures the necessity of time needed to rebuild trust when she writes, "Unfortunately trust isn't a destination we reach; it's a path we walk. Every single day."[187] Psych Central provided a consensus that it takes at least "18-24 months" to repair and rebuild trust.[188] But as we have learned; it is a lifelong journey that unfolds every day.

TALKING

Dr. Gary Chapman, in his book Now You're Speaking My Language, revealed that when divorced couples were asked why their marriage failed, 86 percent replied, "Deficient communication."[189] If this percentage is true, we can clearly understand the paramount importance of talking and communicating. Trust will continue to grow where clear, kind, and honest communication occurs daily.

Effective communication requires both spouses to engage in talking and active listening. Active listening is a conscious effort in which a listener intentionally focuses on fully understanding the message being communicated. Stephen Covey succinctly captured the process when he wrote, "Most people do not listen with the intent to understand, they listen with the intent to reply;"[190]

How important is having an intimate conversation with your spouse when rebuilding trust? Psychologist Willard Harley identified the 10 most common emotional needs of individuals in partner relationships (Harley, 2001), and among these was the need for "intimate conversation."[191]

Good communication between spouses occurs when each partner endeavors not only to lean into the ideas and thoughts of the other but also to demonstrate a willingness to accept and trust their thoughts, though they may, at times, be diametrically opposite to their own.

TRANSFORMATION

In any relationship, the observable transformation of the offending spouse is critical to rebuilding trust. The offended spouse faces the challenge of trusting again, and if there is no transformation in the life of the offending spouse, the viability of trust being rebuilt is extremely low, if not impossible. For example, if the offending spouse declares that he or she is not texting the former lover but texts are later discovered on their phone, trust has been sabotaged once again.

Transformation often requires immediate action in some scenarios, while in others, it moves slowly but progressively toward a communicated goal. For example, an offending spouse might declare that they are looking for another job to avoid working at the same company as their former lover. When the offended spouse sees this transition taking place, they immediately recognize that the offending spouse is sincerely working to build trust. The adage, "Actions speak louder than words" captures the essence of the transformation process.

Jesus, when talking to a woman caught in the very act of adultery, exemplified this principle. He forgave her but simultaneously demanded change (transformation) when He admonished her to "Go and sin no more" (John 8:11, KJV).

HUMILITY

Steven Covey, in his book *Principle-Centered Leadership,* commented that principles 4, 5, and 6 required the tremendous sacrifice of a broken and contrite spirit. He referenced an experience he had observing a marriage plagued by frequent arguments. One thought came to his mind, "These two people must have a broken and contrite spirit toward each other, or this union will never last."[192]

If a marriage characterized by constant arguing demands a broken and contrite spirit, then how much more are those qualities necessary in a marriage where trust has been fractured by infidelity?

Two significant passages in Scripture speak of humility. Jesus said, "Come to Me, all you who labor and are heavy laden, and I will give you rest. Take My yoke upon you and learn from Me, for I am gentle and lowly of heart, and you will find rest for your souls. For My yoke is easy and My burden is light" (Matthew 11:28-30, NKJV). The second scripture found in Philippians 2:1-11, NKJV is a little lengthy, but I have chosen to quote the entire segment.

> Therefore, if there is any consolation in Christ, if any comfort of love, if any fellowship of the spirit, if any affection and mercy, fulfill my joy by being like-minded having the same love, being of one accord of one mind. Let nothing be done through selfish ambition or conceit, but in lowliness of mind that each esteem others better than himself. That each of you look out not only for his own interests but also for the interests of others. Let this mind be in you, which was also in Christ Jesus, who, being in the form of God, did not consider it robbery to be equal with God, but made himself of nor reputation, taking the form of a bondservant, and coming in the likeness of men. And being found in the appearance as a man, he humbled himself and became obedient to the point of death, even the death of the cross. Therefore, God also hath highly exalted him, and given him a name which is above every name. At the name of Jesus every knee should bow, of those in heaven, and of those on earth, and those under

the earth, And that every tongue should confess that Jesus Christ is Lord to the glory of God the Father.

David Benner and Petter Hill. quoting Kinzer (1980, p. 69), provided the following definition of humility: "To be humble means to put the interests and needs of others before your own, and to put yourself at others' disposal as a servant."[193] Humility flies in the face of those who seek to be independent and self-sufficient.

We can simply look at Christ's example when he knelt and washed the disciple's feet, including those of Judas, who would betray Him. His teaching further underscores this principle: "But he who is greatest among you shall be your servant. And he who exalts himself will be humbled and he who humbles himself will be exalted" (Matthew 21:11-12, NKJV).

Saint Augustine wrote, "It was pride that changed angels into devils; it is humility that makes men as angels."[194] Another beautiful quote comes from Simone Weil, who wrote, "Humility is attentive patience."[195]

It takes humility for a spouse who has been unfaithful to confess their sin, and it takes humility for the innocent spouse to refrain from comparing their virtue of faithfulness with the unfaithfulness of the offending spouse. The innocent spouse who forgives and works hard to rebuild trust understands what it means to humble oneself and begin to serve the other. Likewise, the offending spouse knows what it is to humble themselves, take responsibility for their actions and humbly confess their sin.

Humility leaves no room for criticism, contempt, defensiveness, bitterness, justification, rationalization, inflammatory words, comparison, condemnation, or blame.

HONOR

Gary Thomas wrote, "We are called to honor someone even when we know only too well their deepest character flaws."[196] Regardless of whether it is the husband or the wife who has committed sexual betrayal, honor must still be bestowed upon each other.

Paul encouraged the Christians in Rome to "Love one another with brotherly affection. Outdo one another in showing honor" (Romans 12:10, ESV). Douglass Moo explains that the Greek word for "outdoing" one another can have two possible meanings. It may suggest that one goes before or demonstrates the way to someone else and may be understood to surpass another Christian in showing or demonstrating honor. Or it may be interpreted as considering another brother or sister in Christ better than or above oneself.[197]

This is significant. It highlights, in a very practical way, the value and respect one has for their spouse. Honor reflects the fact that every human being has been created in the image of God. While one cannot change the past betrayal, one can change their attitude and consciously choose to bestow honor on a spouse who has repented of the infidelity.

In a marriage where trust has been violated, such a bestowal of honor must be reciprocal. Simon Peter emphasizes the broader significance of honoring and valuing people created in the image of God when he exhorts Christians to "Honor everyone" (I Peter 2:17, ESV).

PATIENCE

Mirriam-Webster defines *patience* as, "Bearing pains, or trials calmly or without complaint, manifesting forbearance under provocation or strain, not hasty or impetuous, steadfast despite opposition, difficulty, or adversity."[198] As you rebuild trust, there must be an abundance of patience.

Jean -Jacques Rousseau wrote, "Patience is bitter, but its fruit is sweet."[199] There will certainly be challenging times, emotional moments, and periods of frustration as you work to rebuild trust. However, if both of you are committed to giving one hundred percent, the effort will be well worth the investment.

The biblical perspective of patience may provide guidance for you as you move forward. The Greek word *hupomone* embraces the concept of endurance or steadfastness. *Hupo* is defined as "under," and *meno* as "to abide." It refers to a spiritual fortitude that enables a Christian to bear up under the weight of a particular circumstance. It is described as "patience, endurance as to things or circumstances."[200]

The Apostle Paul highlighted patience as a spiritual characteristic of the Thessalonians, closely tied to their hope, which may have been associated with the second coming of the Lord Jesus Christ. "Remembering without ceasing your work of faith, and labour of love and patience of hope in our Lord Jesus Christ, in the sight of God and our Father; Knowing, brethren beloved, your election of God" (I Thessalonians 1:3-4, KJV).

The betraying spouse often feels irritated, frustrated, discouraged, and angry during the rebuilding process. However, it is essential to understand that rebuilding trust cannot be rushed. Just as it would be foolish to walk on freshly poured concrete ten minutes after it is laid, it is equally unwise to expect an instant renewal of trust.

Concrete hardens incrementally. Within the first 24-48 hours, it becomes strong enough to walk on; after 7 days, it can support a car; and after 28 days, it can bear the weight of heavy equipment.[201] Similarly, the process of rebuilding trust is incremental and requires extraordinary patience. The deeper the wound, the longer the process will take.

RELIABILITY

The success rate of the rockets from the Falcon 9 family over the past fourteen years from Cape Canaveral is 99.26.[202] When a couple seeks to rebuild trust in their marriage following infidelity, reliability serves as the Cape Canaveral launchpad. No couple will be one hundred percent successful, but the goal should be to get as close as possible in their efforts to launch a renewed relationship. Reliability means each partner commits to doing what they say they will do. While both must strive for reliability, the greater pressure of performance will fall on the offending party.

Solomon, with his great wisdom, declared, "Like a broken tooth or a lame foot is reliance on the unfaithful in a time of trouble" Proverbs 25:9 NIV). Couples must also recognize the indispensable need for grace in this process.

Reliability is substantially real and tangible. For example, if you invite a friend to come in out of the cold and have a cup of hot coffee, they might enter your home, and after five to ten minutes, begin to smell the coffee. This gives them the confidence that the coffee is coming.

Similarly, when a spouse consistently does what they say they will do, it's like "smelling the coffee." You notice them spending time with the children, fulfilling responsibilities, keeping promises, and being transparently and consistently accountable. Such dependable behavior goes a long way in rebuilding trust. Conversely, failing to be reliable in the small things undermines the trust you are working so hard to rebuild.

Perhaps you are on your way in the journey of anticipating reconciliation and a willingness to trust again. Remember, trust that was voluntarily and lovingly given was also voluntarily and resolutely broken. It must now be earned through being responsible, dependable, and reliable. Yet, even as it is earned, trust remains a treasured gift that is given—though, due to the betrayal, it is now given with a greater aspect of uncertainty.

Dr. Lee H. Baucom aptly wrote, "Trust is a two-way street: one person does trustworthy actions, the other person trusts. It requires both."[203]

A spouse who has violated the sacred marriage covenant and seeks to become reliable must shift their focus from themselves to their offended spouse. Failure to prioritize the needs and emotions of their partner may have been a contributing factor to the infidelity. Making this shift may also be the path to healing.

AFFIRMATION

Speaking words of affirmation to a heart that has been emotionally crushed by infidelity is like offering cold water to a man dying of thirst. Positive words hold incredible power, as referenced in Proverbs 18:21, "Death and life are in the power of the tongue: and they that love it shall eat the fruit thereof" (KJV). The Amplified Bible affirms this truth: "Death and life are in the power of the tongue, and those who love it and indulge it will eat its fruit and bear the consequences of their words" (Proverbs 18:21, Amplified Bible).

I encourage you to abundantly offer positive words of affirmation to the spouse you have crushed. However, these words must be both honest and heartfelt. Affirming your love for your spouse will undoubtedly be challenging, but such affirmation is essential for rebuilding trust and connection.

Affirmation from the innocent spouse is paramount for the betraying spouse when a couple is seeking reconciliation. Such affirmation recognizes that your spouse has good qualities despite the crushing betrayal. For example, your spouse may have been a good provider for the family, shown love for the children, or humbly acknowledged his betrayal. Offering affirmation to your offending spouse will be both challenging and necessary

If you are the betrayed spouse, you can also begin to speak words of self-affirmation. Such self-affirmation delves into the depth of your self-worth. A spouse's infidelity does not define who you are. Write some words of self-affirmation and place them somewhere visible to remind yourself of your value each day.

This same process of self-affirmation can also benefit the offending spouse. He or she possesses self-worth regardless of their failure. Practicing self-affirmation in either scenario helps to rewire the negative neural pathways of the brain. "The positive psychology practice of self-affirmation aims to help people combat negative beliefs and restore trust in themselves—or simply like themselves again."[204]

ACCENTUATE POSITIVE EXPERIENCES

As you work to rebuild trust in your marriage and navigate the many challenges you may be facing, it is important to accentuate the positive experiences you observe taking place. For example, this could include noticing the kind words you have received, the improved quality of time spent together, or recognizing that your spouse is actively present in conversations. It may also be reflected in nonsexual affection, such as holding hands or receiving genuine hugs throughout the day.

ACKNOWLEDGE EMOTIONS YOU ARE PROCESSING

Remember, your healing is a journey, not a destination. Each spouse may be navigating a range of emotions. Perhaps there is still anger over the betrayal or fear that trust will be broken again. No two couples experience the same emotions, and your feelings are both valid and important to communicate. Each spouse must allow the other to express their emotions without fear of condemnation. As specific emotions are shared, they can be addressed with laser-focused attention and sincere empathy from the other spouse.

ADDRESS TRIGGERS

While rebuilding trust, it is not uncommon for triggers to intrude upon the reconciliation process. Identifying such triggers is crucial. For example, a wife preparing for work might notice an outfit she was wearing when she discovered the betrayal, causing her to suddenly break down and cry. Similarly, a husband driving to work might notice the same make and model of the car driven by the woman complicit in the infidelity, and his thoughts of her begin to overwhelm his mind.

In some cases, such as clothing, the trigger may be easily removed. In other cases, such as preventing people from driving the identical make and model of a car it may be impossible to eliminate the trigger. Countless triggers may arise, and a spouse must intellectually acknowledge them and then emotionally and courageously dismiss them.

AVOID CONTINUAL SURVEILLANCE

Since trust is, as we mentioned, a very fragile thing, a spouse may feel the need to continually maintain surveillance on their partner. However, if your spouse has been honest with you and there are no circumstances or situations indicating a breach of the trust that is being rebuilt, then it is wise to suspend surveillance. Continual surveillance communicates ongoing distrust and undermines the very trust you are endeavoring to rebuild.

AVOID IMPLEMENTING RIGID RULES

We have seen the importance of establishing good and reasonable boundaries, but implementing rigid rules is an entirely different matter. For example, insisting that the offending spouse abstain from all social media can be overly restrictive, especially since social media can sometimes provide valuable information, such as details about events. Your spouse is not a child who needs constant monitoring; they are an adult who needs to be responsible while being trusted.

Another example would be stringently limiting the amount of money your spouse can spend. Emergencies may arise that require additional funds, making such rigid rules impractical. In his book, *Betrayal and Forgiveness,* Dr. Bruce Chalmer stated, "No matter what rules you get your partner to agree to, you know that they can violate them if they choose. The rules don't protect you. And if you actually trust your partner, you don't need rules."[205]

TAKE TIME TO CONNECT

This is a no-brainer but is perhaps one of the most challenging aspects of rebuilding trust for some. One or both spouses may still be emotionally hurting and doubting the possibility of reconciliation. Amid the emotional pain and uncertainty, it is crucial to take the time to emotionally connect.

This emotional connection may take you back to the moments when you first connected and built your relationship. Such time is critical and should be spent alone with each other, free from the presence of friends, family members, or children. Remember, you are in the process of rebuilding trust.

The time you spend alone with each other should be very deliberate. Do your best to eliminate distractions from cell phones and computers. Turn your attention away from screens and focus on the face of your spouse. Prioritize your marriage by freeing yourself from unnecessary responsibilities that can wait.

PRACTICAL DEMONSTRATIONS OF REBUILDING TRUST

Rebuilding trust can be facilitated through practical demonstrations of commitment and connection. For example, some couples choose to purchase new wedding rings, plan a second honeymoon, or renew their vows. Others may revisit the place where they first met, spend the day there, take pictures, and create lasting memories. Additionally, couples can establish new routines together, such as pizza Fridays, Saturday breakfasts, evening walks, or morning jogs.

TAKE TIME FOR PERSONAL GROWTH

No marriage is perfect, and the painful experience of infidelity glaringly affirms the truth. What are some deficient areas in your life that may have contributed to the infidelity and need to change? These may be areas that were ignored or rationalized.

It might involve developing a greater cognitive awareness of your spouse's physical and sexual needs or gainging a deeper understanding of each other's frustrations. It could mean improving your communication style or sharing your unfulfilled yet realistic expectations.

Perhaps it involves setting physical goals like losing weight, getting more sleep, cutting back on excessive sleep, or incorporating regular exercise into your routine. It might also mean addressing psychological struggles with low self-esteem, self-blame, pride, arrogance, jealousy, shame, or guilt. Additionally, it could involve overcoming self-destructive habits such as substance abuse, excessive alcohol consumption, pornography, or overeating.

It may be your spiritual growth, which could be *the most significant change* in your life. The Westminster Shorter Confession asks the profound question, "What is the chief end of man?" The answer is, "Man's chief end is to glorify God, and to enjoy him forever."[206]

Solomon wrote, "Let us hear the conclusion of the whole matter: Fear God, and keep his commandments: for this the whole duty of man" (Ecclesiastes 12:13, KJV). Reflecting on the purpose of man, A.W. Tozer stated, "Our whole purpose as created beings is that we should utilize our time in delighting in the manifest presence of our Creator."[207]

This journey begins with discovering and understanding that man was created in the image of God to have fellowship with Him. However, man sinned against God in the

Garden of Eden, and God redeemed fallen humanity by sending His only Son, Jesus Christ, to die on the cross of Calvary. Paul so eloquently explained this redemption in Christ, writing, "In him, we have redemption through his blood, the forgiveness of sins, in accordance with the riches of God's grace that he lavished on us" (Ephesians 1:7-8, NIV).

When you find reconciliation with God through Christ, all your past sins are forgiven, and God declares you righteous. You discover the peace you have been searching for your entire life. Billy Graham dogmatically declared, "Peace can be experienced only when we have received pardon—when we have been reconciled to God and when we have harmony within, with our fellow man and especially with God."[208]

You can continue moving forward in reconciling your marriage and rebuilding trust. You can have a marriage built on a solid spiritual foundation. While the scars of infidelity may still exist emotionally or physically, remember that scars point to healing. For example, a six-inch scar on your arm may remind you of a severe accident where you bled and experienced pain. The scar reminds you of the past but also indicates that physical healing has occurred—the wound has healed, and the pain has gone. Unlike physical healing, emotional healing may take much longer and may never reach one hundred percent.

This new foundational spiritual experience of redemption has been described as being "born again," a term used by Christ when speaking to Nicodemus. Jesus emphasized to Nicodemus the necessity of spiritual birth (regeneration) to enter the kingdom of God. New birth, or being "born again," occurs when the supernatural power of the Holy Spirit enters your life and transforms the moral fabric of your being.

You now have a new rule of life in which Christ is the center. Peter Scazzero pointed out that the word "rule" is derived from the Greek word for trellis. A trellis helps a grapevine lift off the ground, allowing it to grow upward and become more fruitful and productive.[209]

You (and your marriage) can become more fruitful and productive because you are no longer enslaved by the power of sin. Your heart—the center of your personality—has been transformed. Jesus taught that out of the heart come "evil thoughts—murder, adultery, sexual immorality, theft, false testimony, and slander" (Matthew 15:19, NIV).

The Apostle Paul referred to these as "the acts of the flesh." He wrote, "The acts of the flesh are obvious: sexual immorality, impurity and debauchery; idolatry and witchcraft; hatred, discord, jealousy, fits of rage, selfish ambition, dissensions, factions, and envy, drunkenness orgies and the like. I warn you, as I did before, that those who live like this will not inherit the Kingdom of God" (Galatians 5:10-21, NIV).

The above passages of Scripture reveal that the fruit of sin exists because of the root of sin. The sinful behaviors we exhibit, such as adultery and sexual immorality, come from our sinful nature. While this does not excuse the exercise of our free will in committing these sins, it does point to their source.

When the Holy Spirit enters our lives, the power of sin is broken, and we are no longer enslaved to it. It is like a light switch—when the switch is turned off, it breaks the flow of the electricity to the fixture. Similarly, as we walk by faith, we yield to the Holy Spirit and not to sin. This is spiritual freedom!

However, even though the Holy Spirit lives within us, we still can yield to sin. The Apostle John certainly recognized the possibility and wrote, "If we confess our sins, he is faithful and just to forgive us our sins and purify us from all unrighteousness" (I John 1:9, NIV).

As Christians, we must be intentional every day in our spiritual walk to yield to the power of the Spirit. This requires immersing ourselves in the Word of God, living a life of prayer, and connecting with other members of the body of Christ in community. These practices are essential for spiritual growth and sustained freedom.

NOTES

1. https://www.sabinorecovery.com/can-cheating-cause-ptsd/#:~:text=In%20some%20cases%2C%20the%20impact,reminds%20you%20of%20the%20affair.

2. Linda S. Mintle, *Divorce Proofing Your Marriage.* (Lake Mary: Siloam A Strang Company, 2001), 183.

3. Cindy Bell, *Healing Your Marriage When Trust is Broken: Finding Forgiveness and Restoration* (Eugene: Harvest House Publishers, 2011), 49.

4. Kathy Nickerson, *The Courage to Stay: How to Heal from An Affair & Save Your Marriage,* (Laguna Beach: K Press, 2022), 2.

5. Douglas E. Rosenau *A Celebration of Sex: A Guide to Enjoying God's Gift of Sexual Intimacy* (Nashville: Thomas Nelson, 2022),347.

6. Archibald D. Hart & Sharon May Hart, *Safe Haven Marriage*: *Building a Relationship You Want to Come Home To.* (Nashville: W Publishing Group, 2003), 114).

7. David G. Benner & Peter C. Hill (Eds). *Baker Encyclopedia of Psychology and Counseling* (Grand Rapids: Baker Books 1999), 392.

8. Jeanie Allen, *Untangle Your Emotions*: *Naming What You Feel and Knowing What to Do About It* (Colorado Springs: Waterbrook, 2024), 40.

9. Peter Scazzero, *Emotionally Healthy Spirituality* (Grand Rapids: Zondervan, 2017), 24.

10. Pierce J. Howard, *The Owner's Manual for The Brain: Everyday Applications from Mind-Brain Research, Third Edition.* (Austin: Bard Press, 2006) 321.

11. Ibid, 321-322.

12. Gary Chapman, *Anger: Taming A Powerful Emotion* (Chicago: Moody Press, 2015), 18.

13. Christopher Ash and Steve Midgley, *The Heart of Anger* (Wheaton: Crossway, 2021), 25.

14. James Dobson, *Emotions Can You Trust Them?* (Grand Rapids: Revell, 1975), 105.

15. Gary Chapman, *One More Try*: *What to Do when Your Marriage is Falling Apart* (Chicago: Moody Press 2014), 110.

16. (Author Unknown https://brainyquote.com).

17. Rona B. Subotnik and Gloria G. Harris, *Surviving Infidelity*: *Making Decisions, Recovering from the Pain,* (Avon: Adam, Media 2005), 105-106.

18. David G. Benner &Peter C. Hill (Eds). *Baker Encyclopedia of Psychology and Counseling* (Grand Rapids: Baker Books 1999), 654.

19. Pierce J. Howard, *The Owner's Manual for The Brain: Everyday Applications from Mind-Brain Research.* (Austin: Bard Press 2006), 321.

20. https://www.brainyquote.com/lists/topics/top-10-jealousy-quotes

21. https://www.psychologytoday.com/us/blog/insight-is-2020/201409/3-prime-reasons-why-people-get-jealous

22. *https://www.brainyquote.com/topics/bitterness*-quotes

23. Tim Clinton and Diane Langberg, *Counseling Women* (Grand Rapids: Baker Books, 2011), 82.

24. Shirley P. Glass with Jean Coppock Staeheli, *Not "Just Friends"*: *Rebuilding Trust and Recovering Your Sanity After Infidelity* (New York: Atria Paperback, 2020),56.

25. Shawn Johnson, *Attacking Anxiety*: *From Panicked and Depressed to Alive and Free*, (Nashville: Nelson, 2022), 42.

26. Dave Carder & Duncan Jaenicke, *Torn Asunder: Recovering from an Extramarital Affair* (Chicago: Moody Publishers, 2008), 175.

27. Kevin Skinner, *Treating Trauma from Sexual Betrayal* (Lindon: KSkinner Corp: 2017), 34.

28. James Dobson, Emotions Can You Trust Them? (Grand Rapids: Revell, 2014) 18, 25.

29. Ibid, 17.

30. Shirley P. Glass with Jean Coppock Staeheli, *Not "Just Friends"*: Rebuilding Trust and Recovering Your Sanity After Infidelity (New York: Atria Paperback, 2020), 256.

31. Heather Daveduik Gingrich, *Restoring the Shattered Self: A Christian Counselor's Guide to Complex Trauma* (Downers Grove: InterVarsity Press, 2020), 137.

32. Shirley P. Glass and Jean Coppock Staeheli *Not "Just Friends"*: Rebuilding Trust and Recovering Your Sanity After Infidelity (New York: Atria Paperback, 2020), 40.

33. Amanda Aliff, *Infidelity Journal: For the Partner Who Has Betrayed* (Columbia: Amazon, 2022), 8.

34. Ibid. p. 8.

35. https://www.sabinorecovery.com/can-cheating-cause ptsd/#:~:text=In%20some%20cases%2C%20the%20 impact,reminds%20you%20of%20the%20affair.

36. https://www.merriam-webster.com

37. Steven Tracy, *Mending of the Soul* (Grand Rapids: Zondervan, 2005), 74.

38. Edward T. Welch, *Shame Interrupted* (Greensboro: New Growth Press, 2012), 2.

39. Curt Thompson, *The Soul of* Shame (Downers Grove: IVP Books, 2005), 23

40. Dr Kathy Nickerson, *The Courage to Stay: How to Heal From An Affair and Save Your Marriage* (Lake Forest: Dr. Kathy & Company Press, 2022), 203-204.

41. Michelle Mays, *The Betrayal Bind* (Las Vegas: Central Recovery Press, 2023),75-76.

42. A.W. Tozer, *The Essential Tozer Collection* (Bloomington: Bethany House, 2013) 27.

43. Dutch Sheets, *Becoming Who You Are* (Bloomington: Bethany House, 2010), 33.

44. Clinton and Langberg, *Counseling Women* (Grand Rapids: Baker Books, 2011), 139.

45. Ibid, 140.

46. Ibid, 189.

47. American Psychiatric Association, *Diagnostic and Statistical Manual of Mental Disorders* (Washington: American Psychiatric Association Publishing, 2013), 189.

48. Max Lucado, *Anxious for Nothing* (Nashville: Thomas Nelson, 2017), 5.

49. https://www.merriam-webster.com/dictionary/panic#:~:text=%3A%20a%20sudden%20overpowering%20fright,often%20accompanied%20by%20mass%20oflight

50. Pierce J, Howard, *The Owner's Manual for The Brain*: Everyday Applications for Mind-Brain Research. (Austin: Bard Press, 2006), 431-432.

51. Ibid, 431.

52. Linda Mintle, *Letting Go of Worry*: God's Plan for Finding Peace and Contentment (Eugene: Harvest House Publishers, 2011), 64.

53. https://www.poetryfoundation.org/collections/101598/poems-about-loneliness-and-solitude

54. https://www.psychologytoday.com/us/basics/loneliness

55. Lysa Terkeurst, *I Want to Trust You but I Don't*: Moving Forward When You're Skeptical of Others, Afraid of What God Woll Allow, and Doubtful of Your Own Discernment (Nashville: Nelson Books 2024), 78

56. James Dobson, *Love Must Be Tough: New Hope for Marriages in Crisis* (Carol Stream: Tyndale Momentum, 2007), 27.

57. Kevin Skinner, *Treating Trauma from Sexual Betrayal* (Lindon: KSkinner Corp, 2017), 142.

58. Gary Smalley, *The DNA of Relationships*: Discover How You Are Designed for Satisfying Relationships (Carol Stream: Tyndale House Publishers, 2007), 18.

59. Lewis B. Smedes, *Forgive and Forget*: Healing the Hurts We Don't

Deserve (New York: Harper One, 1994), 21.

60. Shirley P. Glass and Jean Coppock Staeheli, *Not "Just Friends": Rebuilding Trust and Recovering Your Sanity After Infidelity* (New York: Atria Paperback, 2020), 127.

61. Lewis B. Smedes, *Forgive & Forget: Healing the Hurts We Don't Deserve* (New York: Harper One, 1996), 133.

62. https://www.merriam-webster.com/dictionary/revenge#:~:text=transitive%20verb-,1,revenge%20an%20insult

63. Ibid.

64. https://www.psychologytoday.com/us/blog/transcending-the-past/202311/revenge-is-rarely-sweet

65. Tim Clinton & Dr. Mark Laaser, *Sexuality & Relationship Counseling* (Grand Rapids: Baker Books, 2010) 44.

66. Dan B. Allender, *Healing the Wounded Heart: The Heartache of Sexual Abuse and the Hope of Transformation* (Grand Rapids: Baker Book, 2016), 59.

67. Pierce J. Howard, *The Owner's Manual for The Brain: Everyday Applications from Mind-Brain Research* (Austin: Bard Press, 2006), 817

68. Ibid, 817

69. Ibid.

70. Peter Scazzero, *Emotionally Healthy Spirituality* (Grand Rapids: Zondervan, 2017), 49,

71. Esther Perel, *The State of Affairs: Rethinking Infidelity* (New York: Harper, 2017.31

72. Linda S. Mintle, *Divorce Proofing Your Marriage* (Lake Mary: Siloam, 2001), 182.

73. Lee H. Baucom, *Recovering from the Affair: Your Guide to Saving Your Marriage After Emotional Or Physical Infidelity* (Louisville: Aspire Publishing, 2017), 8.

74. Michelle Mays, *The Betrayal Bind: How to Heal When the Person You Love the Most Hurts You The Most* (Las Vegas: Central Recovery Press, 2023), 30.

75. Michele Weiner-Davis, *Healing from Infidelity: The Divorce Busting Guide to Rebuilding Your Marriage After an Affair.* (Woodstock: Michele Weiner-Davis Training Corporation, 2017)20.

76. Michelle Mays, *The Betrayal Bind: How to Heal When the Person You love the Most Hurts You the Worst,* (Las Vegas: Central Recovery Press, 2023), 4.

77. Linda Mintle, *Divorce Proofing Your Marriage.* (Mary: Siloam, 2001), 186.

78. Lee H. Baucom, *Recovering from the Affair: Your Marriage Guide to Saving Your Marriage After Emotional Or Physical Infidelity,* (Louisville: Aspire Publishing, 2017), 8.

79. Esther Perel, *The State of Affairs: Rethinking Infidelity,* (New York: Harper, 2017), 31.

80. Shirley P. Glass, *"Not Just Friends: Rebuilding Trust and Your Sanity After Infidelity*, (New York: Atria Paperback, 2020), 56

81. Rona B. Subbotnik and Gloria G. Harris, *Surviving Infidelity: Making Decisions, Recovering from the Pain,* (Avon: Adams Media, 2005), 18.

82. Ami Rokach and Sybil H. Chan, "Love and Infidelity: Causes and Consequences," *International Journal of Environmental Research and Public Health,* 2023 Mar;20(5): 3904. https://www.ncbi.nim.gov/pmc/articles/PMC10002055/#:text=infidelity%20causes%20grief%20and%20rlational42%2c692C70%5D.

83. Shirely P. Glass, *Not Just Friends: Rebuilding Trust and Recovering Your Sanity After Infidelity,* (New York: Atria Paperback, 2020), 380.

84. Jennifer P. Schneider, *Back from Betrayal: Recovering From His Affairs,* (Tucson: Recover Resources Press, 2005), 113.

85. Psychologytoday.com/us/blog/strictly-causual20142.

86. Ted Shimer, *The Freedom Fight: The New Drug and the Truths that Set Us Free,* (Houston: High Bridge Books, 2020), 16.

87. Ibid, 16.

88. Bev Hislop, *Shepherding Women in Pain: Real Women, Real Issues, and What You Need to Know to Truly Help* (Chicago: Moody Publishers, 2010), 254.

89. David G Benner & Peter C. Hill (EDS), *Baker Encyclopedia of Psychology & Counseling* (Grand Rapids: Baker Books, 1999), 883.

90. Ibid, 883

91. Judith A. Reisman, *Sexual Sabotage: How One Mad Scientist Unleashed a Plague of Corruption and Contagion on America*

(Washington, DC: WMD Books, 2010), 169.

92. Sam Black, *The Healing Church: What Churches Get Wrong About Pornography* (New York: Morgan James Publishing, 2023), 36.

93. Mark R. Laaser, *Healing the Wounds of Sexual Addiction* (Grand Rapids: Zondervan, 2004), 32.

94. Clifford & Joyce Penner, *The Gift of Sex: A Guide to Sexual Fulfillment,* (Nashville: Thomas Nelson, 2003), 312.a

95. https://www.emotionalaffair.org/silent-infidelity-how-porn-addiction-affects-your-marriage/

96. Ibid,

97. Ted Shimer, *The Freedom Fight: The New Drug and the Truths that Set Us Free* (Houston, High Bridge Books, 2020), 70.

98. Ibid, 66.

99. Bev Hislop, *Shepherding Women in Pain: Real Women, Real Issues, and What You Need to Know to Truly Help* (Chicago: Moody Publisher, 2010), 254-255.

100. Archibald D. Hart & Sharon May, *Safe Haven Marriage: Building a Relationship You Can Come Home To* (Nashville: W. Publishing Group 2003), 178.

101. Dr. James Dobson, *Complete Marriage and Family Home Reference Guide.* (Carol Stream: Tyndale Momentum, 2000), 385.

102. https://www.paradisecreekrecoverycenter.com/porn-addiction-to-infidelity

103. Ted Shimer, *The Freedom Fight: The New Drug and ghe Truths That Set Us Free* (Houston: High Bridge Books, 2020), 31

104. Ibid, 30.

105. https://www.psychologytoday.com/us/blog/love-digitally/201601/what-your-sexting-really-reveals

106. https://www.choosingtherapy.com/is-sexting-cheating/

107. Ibid.

108. https://www.psychologytoday.com/us/blog/urban-survival/201904/nonconsensual-sexting-linked-anxiety-and-depression

109. https://drkarenfinn.com

110. Kathy Nickerson, *The Courage to Stay: How to Heal from Affair & Save Your Marriage* (Laguna Beach: Kay Press, 2022), 251.

111. Michele Weimer-Davis, *Healing from Infidelity.* (Woodstock: Michele Weimer-Davis Training Corporation 2017),23.

112. Michelle Mays, *The Betrayal Bind: How to Heal When he Person You Love the Most Hurts You the Mos* (Las Vegas: Central Recovery Press, 2023), 309.

113. https://lesley.edu/about/faculty-staff-directory/brian-becker

114. Cindy Beall, *Healing Your Marriage When Trust Is Broken*: *Finding Forgiveness and Restoration* (Eugene: Harvest House Publishers, 2011), 91.

115. Gary Chapman, *When Sorry Isn't Enough: Making Things Right with Those You Love* (Chicago: Northfield Publishing, 2013) 22.

116. Alexandra Katehakis, *Erotic Intelligence*: *Igniting Hot Healthy Sex While in Recovery from Sex Addiction* (Deerfield Beach: Health Communications, Inc. 2010), 6.

117. https://www.pixartprinting.co.uk/blog/empathy-quotations/

118. Joel P. Bretscher & Kenneth C. Haugk, *The Gift of Empathy: Helping others Feel Valued, Cared For and Understood* (St. Louis: Stephen Ministries, 2023),15.

119. https://ofhsoupkitchen.org/empathy-quotes

120. Steven Covey, https://brainyquote.com.

121. *Baker Encyclopedia of Psychology & Counseling* (Grand Rapids: Baker Books, 1999), 398.

122. Ibid, 398.

123. Steven Covey, *The 7 Habits of Highly Effective People* (New York: Simon & Schuster, 2020), 278.

124. Ibid, 279.

125. https://pmc.ncbi.nlm.nih.gov/articles/PMC3156001/

126. https://www.youtube.com/watch?v=PU0QOKIPU90

127. Ibid

128. https://www.brainyquote.com/quotes/robert_h_schuller_156006

129. https://www.merriam-webster.com/dictionary/hope#:~:text=noun,1,expectation%20of%20fulfillment%20or%20success

130. Ibid.

131. *Baker Encyclopedia of Psychology & Counseling* (Grand Rapids: Baker Books, 1999), 578.

132. https://www.google.com/search?client=safari&rls=en&q=American+Psychological+Assoiciation+definition+of+hope&ie=UTF-8&oe=UTF-8

133. Rona B. Subotnik & Gloria B. Harris, *Surviving Infidelity: Making Decisions, Recovering from the Pain* (Avon: Adams Media, 2005) 87-88.

134. Ibid, 87-88.

135. W. L. Seaver, *Prayer: Communication with God in Everything—Collected Insights from A W. Tozer.* (Chicago: Moody Publishers, 2016), 40.

136. https://www.linkedin.com/pulse/human-brain-can-only-process-one-thought-time-deepmm

137. Gordon D. Fee, *The New International Commentary on the New Testament*: *Paul's Letter to the Philippians*. (Grand Rapids: Wm. Eerdmans Publishing Company,1995), 415.

138. Kevin Skinner, *Treating Trauma from Sexual* Betrayal: *The Essential Tools for Healing*. (Lindon: KSkinner Corp. 2017) 155.

139. https://dictionary.apa.org/denial

140. Bruce Fisher and Robert Alberti, *Rebuilding When Your Relationships Ends*. (Oakland: Impact Publishers, 2016) 294

141. James Dobson, *Complete Marriage and Family Home Reference Guide.* (Carol Stream: Tyndale Momentum, 2000), 428.

142. Rona B. Subotnik, and Gloria GF Harris, *Surviving Infidelity*: *Making Decisions Recovering from the Pain.* (Avon: Adams Media, 2005), 80.

143. Ibid, 135.

144. Melody Beattie, *Codependent No More*: *How to Stop Controlling Others and Start Caring for Yourself.* (New York: Spiegel and Grau, 2022), 136.

145. https://www.brainyquote.com/topics/confrontation-quotes

146. James Dobson, *Love Must Be Tough: New Hope for Marriages In Crisis*. (Carol Stream: Tyndale Momentum, 2007), 146-147), 146-147.

147. David G. Benner & Peter C. Hill (Eds). *Baker Encyclopedia of Psychology & Counseling*. (Grand Rapids: Baker Book, 1999),894-895.

148. Ibid.

149. David G. Benner & Peter C. Hill (Eds). *Baker Encyclopedia of Psychology & Counseling*. (Grand Rapids: Baker Book, 1999), 468.

150. https://www.psychologytoday.com/us/blog/the-addiction-connection/202310/the-power-of-forgiveness

151. Lewis B Smedes, *Forgive & Forget: Healing the Hurts We Don't Deserve* (New York: Harper One, 1996), 49

152. https://word-counter.com/popular/forgiveness-quotes/?utm_source=google&utm_medium=EAIaIQobChMIwc31_eDghwMVmlz_AR1w9w5nEAAYAiAAEgJp4_D_BwE&cuid=EAIaIQobChMIwc31_eDghwMVmlz_AR1w9w5nEAAYAiAAEgJp4_D_BwE&gad_source=1&gclid=EAIaIQobChMIwc31_eDghwMVmlz_AR1w9w5nEAAYAiAAEgJp4_D_BwE.

153. Cindy Beall, *Healing Your Marriage When Trust Is Broken* (Eugene: Harvest House Publishers, 2011), 101.

154. https://blogs.shu.edu/diplomacyresearch/2013/12/31/martin-luther-king-jr/#:~:text=MLK%20said%3A%20"Forgiveness%20does%20not,a%20barrier%20to%20the%20relationship.

155. Shirley P. Glass, *Not "Just Friends": Rebuilding Trust and Recovering Your Sanity After Infidelity* (New York: Atria, 2020), 119.

156. Michelle Weiner-Davis, *Healing from Infidelity* (Bolder: Michelle-Warner-Davis, 2017), 118.

157. https://www.goodreads.com/quotes/tag/hiding-place

158. Kevin Skinner, *Treating Trauma from Sexual Betrayal: The Essential Tools for Healing* (KSkinner Corp, 2017) 185.

159. Billy Graham, *Peace with God* (Nashville: W Publishing Group, 1984), 283.

160. https://www.psychologytoday.com/us/blog/what-mentally-strong-people-dont-do/201504/7-scientifically-proven-benefits-of-gratitude

161. W. L. Seaver, *Prayer: Communing with God In Everything—Collected Insights from A. W. Tozer* (Chicago: Moody Press, 2016), 88.

162. https://www.psychologytoday.com/us/basics/gratitude

163. https://www.google.com/search?client=safari&rls=en&q=How+many+people+end+up+addicted+to+drugs+yearly+in++the+USA&ie=UTF-8&oe=UTF-8

164. Dallas Willard, *Renovation of the Heart: Putting on the Character of Christ* (Nave Press/Tyndale House Publishers: Carol Stream, 2021), 182.

165. Pierce J. Howard, *The Owner's Manual for The Brain, Everyday Applications from Mind-Brain Research* (Bard Press: Austin, 2006), 202.

166. Pierce J. Howard, *The Owner's Manual for The Brain: Everyday Applications from Mind Brain Research* (Austin: Bard Press, 2006), 227-228.

167. Ibid, 202

168. https://www.usdairy.com/news-articles/dairy-and-mental-health?https://www.usdairy.com/news-articles/does-protein-give-you- energy&campaignid=21473506499&adgroupid=16 5703048478&keyword=foods%20that%20help%20with%20 stress&device=c&gad_source=1&gbraid=0AAAAAC58wDefSKXX ZBIT1DS11f1brx845&gclid=EAIaIQobChMIu77f47P_iAMVwTjUAR-11CA8sEAAYASAAEgKqFPD_BwE

169. Pierce J. Howard, *The Owner's Manual for The Brain: Everyday Applications from Mind-Brain Research* (Austin: Bard Press, 2006), 823.

170. John C. Thomas & Lisa Sosin, *Therapeutic Expedition: Equipping The Christian Counselor for the Journey* (B&H Publishing Group: Nashville, 2011), 423.

171. Henry Cloud & Dr. John Townsend, *Boundaries: When to Say Yes How to Say No to Take Control of Your Life* (Grand Rapids: Zondervan 2017), 27.

172. Michele Weiner-Davis, *Healing from Infidelity: The Divorce Busting Guide to Rebuilding Your Marriage After an Affair* (Michele Weiner-Davis: 2017), 194.

173. https://www.psychologytoday.com/us/blog/talking-apes/202108/how-social-isolation-affects-intimate-couples

174. http://archives.yalealumnimagazine.com/issues/2008_07/serenity.html

175. Ibid.

176. https://www.paired.com/articles/trust-quotes-for-a-relationship

177. Shirley P. Glass, *Not "Just Friends": Rebuilding Trust and Recovering Your Sanity After Infidelity* (New York: Atria 2003), 12

178. David G. Benner & Peter C. Hill (Eds). *Baker Encyclopedia of Psychology & Counseling.* (Grand Rapids: Baker Book, 1999), 1232.

179. Rona B. Subotnik and Gloria G. Harris, *Surviving Infidelity*: *Making Decisions, Recovering from the Pain* (Avon: Adams Media, 2005),145.

180. Gary Chapman and Jennifer Thomas, *When Sorry Isn't Enough* (Chicago: Northfield Publishing, 2013), 87.

181. Gary Chapman & Jennifer Thomas: The 5 Apology Languages: The Secret to Healthy Relationships (Chicago: Northfield Publishing, 2022) pp. 21-630.

182. Shirley P. Glass, *Not "Just Friends"*: *Rebuilding Trust and Recovering Your Sanity After Infidelity.* (New York: Atria, 2020), 193.

183. https://www.merriam-webster.com/dictionary/trust#:~:text=Synonyms%20of%20trust-,1,in%20which%20confidence%20is%20placed.

184. Caroline Madden, PhD, *After a Good Man Cheats*: *How to Rebuild Trust & Intimacy with Your Wife* (San Marino: Train of Thought Express, 2015), 40.

185. Cindy Beall, *Healing Your Marriage When Trust Is Broken*: *Finding Forgiveness and Restoration* (Eugene: Harvest House Publisher, 2011), 26.

186. Kathy Knickerson, *The Courage to Stay*: *How to Heal From An Affair And Save Your Marriage* (Laguna Beach: K Press, 2021) 104.

187. Cindy Beall, *Healing Your Marriage When Trust is Broken: Finding Forgiveness and Restoration* (Eugene: Harvest House Publishers, 2011), 107.

188. https://psychcentral.com/relationships/rebuilding-a-marriage-after-infidelity#address-ptsd

189. Gary Chapman, *Now You're Speaking My Language: Honest Communication & Deeper Intimacy for A Stronger Marriage* (Nashville: B&H Publishing Group, 2014),5.

190. Steven Covey, *The Seven Habits of Highly Effective People* (New York: Simon & Schuster, 2020), 277.

191. https://www.psychologytoday.com/us/blog/in-it-together/202006/active-listening-skills

192. Steven Covey, *Principle-Centered Leadership* (New York: Simon & Shuster, 90), 92.

193. Pierce J. Howard, *The Owner's Manual for The B*rain: *Everyday Applications from Mind-Brain Research* (Austin: Bard Press, 2006), 591.

194. https://www.brainyquote.com/topics/humility-quotes
195. Ibid
196. Gary Thomas, *Sacred Marriage: What If God Designed Marriage to Make Us Holy More Than To Make Us Happy* (Grand Rapids: Zondervan, 2000), 53.
197. Douglass Moo, *The Epistle to the Romans. The New International Commentary on the New Testament* (Grand Rapids: William B. Eerdmans Publishing Company, 1996), 777.
198. https://www.merriam-webster.com
199. https://www.rd.com/list/quotes-calm/
200. Spiros Zodhiates, *The Complete Word Study of the New Testament*
201. https://renovated.com/concrete-curing-time-chart/
202. https://en.wikipedia.org/wiki/Falcon_9
203. Lee H. Baucom, *Recovering from the Affair* (Louisville: Aspire Publishing, 2017), 118.
204. https://www.psychologytoday.com/us/basics/affirmations
205. Bruce Chalmer, *Betrayal and Forgiveness: How to Navigate the Turmoil and Learn to Trust Again* (Orlando: Someware Publishing, 2024), 128-129).
206. https://thewestminsterstandard.org/westminster-shorter-catechism/
207. A.W. Tozer, *Experiencing the Presence of God: Teachings From The Book of Hebrews* (Ventura: Regal, 2010).
208. Billy Graham, *Peace with God* (Nashville: W Publishing Group, 1985), 280.
209. Peter Scazzero, *Emotionally Healthy Spirituality* (Chicago: Zondervan, 2017), 190.

www.ingramcontent.com/pod-product-compliance
Lightning Source LLC
Chambersburg PA
CBHW060523080526
44586CB00012B/592